4/12

Why Every Man Needs a Tractor

And Other Revelations in the Garden

Why Every Man Needs a Tractor

Charles Elliott

FRANCES LINCOLN LIMITED
PUBLISHERS

Frances Lincoln Limited
4 Torriano Mews
Torriano Avenue
London NW5 2RZ
www.franceslincoln.com

A catalogue record for this book is available from the British Library.

978-0-7112-3239-6

Printed and bound in China

1 2 3 4 5 6 7 8 9

For Carol, still

CONTENTS

Introduction

The stacks of the London Library hold many wonders. There are hundreds of feet of shelving devoted to bound volumes of journals – Sussex Notes and Queries, for instance, or a complete run of The Babylonian and Oriental Record (1886-1901). Other sections hold biography, fiction and history, quite enough of each to keep the speediest reader occupied for several lives. But what I find most delightful is the almost dementedly comprehensive category designated 'Science & Miscellaneous'. Whether or not this was deliberately created as a sort of librarian's cop-out or intellectual sump, or just grew naturally over the course of the 150 years since the library's founding, I wouldn't venture to guess. In any case, it is here under this one heading that you will find books on everything from Sex to Somnambulism, Sewage Disposal to Angling, Treasure Hunting to Boxing. And, of course, Gardening. The array is splendidly eclectic. If all human knowledge isn't (quite) here, no dilettante could ask for more. I certainly couldn't.

As both a regular visitor to 'Science & Miscellaneous' and a gardener, I've often been struck by the fact that gardening offers the same opportunity for multiple approaches. It can be enjoyed in so many ways. You can spend hours digging, weeding and transplanting, or you can merely sit indoors and contemplate – constructively, of course – what might be done when the rain stops. You can delve into serious botany or, if you'd prefer (and I frequently do), you can spend your time randomly browsing books or exploring the improbable riches of the Internet. For the adventurous there are other people's gardens and the pleasures of envy. In short, gardening is a vast and wonderfully varied world, rather like 'Science & Miscellaneous'. I offer this less as an excuse than an explanation for the extremely unfocussed content of this book.

As in earlier collections of these pieces, the hands-on gardener will find very little practical information of use to him here. None, really. Other writers more knowledgeable than I should be consulted for advice on potato blight, honey fungus, and colour-coding your azaleas. On the other hand, if you would like to know something about electro-horticulture, or imaginary plants, or the longevity of seeds, you've come to the right place. The principle at work in this collection is inclusiveness. Or whatever makes (in my judgment) a good story and has something to do with gardening, however tangential. In this connection, along with longer pieces I have included reviews of a few recent books on subjects that will not seem out of place.

Many of these essays have been published previously in several British and American magazines, especially Hortus. I am grateful to the various editors for their accommodating natures, and as usual to the libraries without whose splendid facilities we would all be much poorer – the British Library, and the Lindley Library of the Royal Horticultural Society, and, above all, the London Library.

ECCENTRICITIES

Wired

Ever since Benjamin Franklin got his knuckles burnt when flying a kite in a thunderstorm (why he didn't simply go up in flames remains a mystery), a number of scientists – and even more quacks – have been curious about the possibilities of what has been called electro-horticulture. The logic is inescapable – most things react to an electric current. Why shouldn't plants react too, and perhaps grow better/faster/bigger?

While I'm not prepared to speak authoritatively on this subject in general, I have had a bit of experience with one aspect of electro-horticulture: the use of electric lights – fluorescent lights to be precise – in a contraption intended to start seedlings indoors. I've written about this before. It had three shelves illuminated by bulbs casting a special kind of light (I'm not sure how special it really was) and provided space for a couple of dozen seed trays. At the time I was working on the 29th floor of a New York City office building, and inevitably the contraption ended up in the corridor outside the ladies' room, which was the only place I could find to put it. The plants didn't seem to mind. In fact, under the benevolent rays of the Gro-Lux, watered from time to time, and admired by most of my fellow office workers as they passed by, the infant zucchini, tomatoes, snapdragons, calendulas and the rest thrived. If they resented the low status of their situation, they could at least look forward to being transplanted.

So far as I know, there is no particular controversy about the effectiveness of artificial light in growing plants. It works fine, and can be employed to good purpose even by those who, like me, are only modestly competent in technical matters. But the world of electro-horticulture involves more – and stranger – things than fluorescent tubing. This is where we get into the fun stuff though, as we shall see, it's well to be careful.

Apparently the first man to explore the potential was one Dr Maimbray (or Mainbray or Von Maimbray – sources differ) of Edinburgh who in 1746 undertook to electrify two myrtle bushes. He used a primitive electrostatic generator to produce the power. After being zapped for the entire month of October, according to Maimbray, the shrubs put out new branches and blossomed. A paper on the effects of electricity on vegetables read to the Royal Society in London the following year resulted in a wave of enthusiastic experiments, none of which seem to have come to anything. 'The most striking feature of these experiments', a historian remarked later, 'is that they are *always contradictory*'.

He might have been speaking for succeeding generations of frustrated electro-horticultural researchers, because inconsistency appears to have dogged their efforts from the start. Triumphs were no sooner announced than failures followed. Nevertheless, work continued. The Abbé Pierre Bertholon, a French priest and pioneer electrical researcher, published *De l'Électricité des Vegetaux*, in which he described his method of spraying electrified water on growing crops from a special 'electrovegetometer', thereby encouraging them to grow. Bertholon's machine involved an insulated barrel of water, a wired-up watering can, and a sort of trolley on which the operator stood while trundling along the rows to deliver the charged spray to the plants. Results were ambiguous. In Italy, less ambiguous results were obtained by a Dr Gardini, whose experiments in Turin backfired. Wire netting installed in the previously productive garden of a monastery there reduced its fertility to such an extent that the infuriated monks tore down the apparatus and ejected Dr Gardini. (In fairness, it must be said that Gardini could claim to have proved what he set out to prove – that plants deprived of atmospheric electricity by being covered with fine mesh metal cages would wilt and die. And so they had.)

Given the rudimentary understanding of electricity itself during this period, it is not surprising that scientific opinion about the way it might or might not affect plants was severely divided, if not fragmented. The great Alexander von Humboldt, in a work on plant physiology published in 1794, declared that there was scarcely any subject upon which learned men differed so profoundly. And if you did believe that electricity was important in horticulture, the questions about how and why crowded in. Did it increase fertility? Did it make atmospheric chemicals like nitrogen more available? Did it serve to break up soil particles? Did it make sap move faster inside the plants? What sort of electricity – static or voltaic – was most significant? The puzzles seemed endless.

Meanwhile, theories and experiments multiplied. For centuries farmers had sworn that thunderstorms make crops grow quicker. (Bertholon went so far as to blame the failure of the hop crop in 1787 to a shortage of lightning.) Attempts were made to simulate or trap atmospheric electricity by stringing wires across fields or by erecting high antennae. One researcher maintained that this could be achieved by sticking a conical coil of stiff wire wound with nine turns (clockwise in the Southern Hemisphere, counterclockwise in the Northern) one foot north of a plant. Results, as usual, were mixed, with enthusiasts claiming success and sceptics the opposite.

In the 1840s there was a considerable stir. A Dr Forster, of Findrassie, near Elgin, reported that after stretching wires in particular directions over a crop of barley, he had produced an exceptionally luxuriant crop. Findrassie, I'm forced to note, is only a short distance away from Findhorn, famous a few years back for its supernaturally huge vegetables, but whether or not the location had anything to do with Forster's achievement, it had consequences; fresh trials were projected all over Britain, even in the Royal Horticultural Society gardens at Chiswick. According to John Claudius Loudon, the premier gardening journalist of the day, 'in all cases the result was a complete failure'. But then Loudon never was a believer.

What electro-horticulture did get was plenty of fashionable publicity. One especially delightful story tells of a demonstration conducted by the Marquis of Anglesea at a dinner party. (This noble lord is perhaps best remembered for his exchange with the Duke of Wellington during the battle of Waterloo. Anglesea: 'By God, sir, I've lost my leg!' Wellington: 'By God, sir, so you have!') When the dinner guests sat down they watched cress seeds being sown into flats containing a mixture of sand, manganese oxide and salt, the whole moistened with diluted sulphuric acid and electrified. Five hours later – it was a leisurely dinner – the cress was harvested and served up in a salad. At least that was the way the story went.

Other tactics called for metal plates sunk in the earth to electrify a plot. In the 1840s a New York farmer named William Ross reportedly produced several times the normal yield of a potato patch by burying a 5" x 15" copper plate and a similar zinc plate 200 feet away, linking them with a wire to create a galvanic cell. The development of mains electricity offered new scope for experimentation, along with a certain degree of hazard – in the words of one expert, 'when using alternating current, great care must be taken to prevent electrocution of oneself and the plants'. Undeterred researchers fired away, and in addition to claims of bigger crops reported some interesting and potentially useful side-effects, among them a reduction in harmful insects, bacteria and fungi, as well as speedier seed germination and stratification of grafts. Electricity could also be used to kill weeds.

The years before World War I saw the last real flowering of electro-horticulture, stimulated by the work and writings of several European experimenters. Most important was a Finnish scientist named Karl Selim Lenström, who noticed how rapidly and vigorously plants grew in the short Lapland summer and concluded that, as shown by the *aurora borealis*, it was because there was so much electricity floating in the Arctic air. Lenström strung up current-carrying wires, first over pots and later over whole fields, finally concluding that electricity encouraged everything from parsnips to strawberries (though not turnips and tobacco).

A number of large-scale trials based on Lenström's findings soon began in the US and England. One at least was less than legitimate. In 1901 *The New York Times* reported the misdeeds of Michaelis Quentesky, a New Jersey truck farmer, who had built a network of wires over his radish patch and powered it with electricity stolen from the Bordentown Trolley Company. Quentesky argued that he was simply advancing science, since he was able to bring radishes to marketable size in fourteen days instead of the normal six weeks. *The Times* sympathized – if Quentesky was right, the paper wrote, 'as a discovery it would be worth many fold the value of all the current of the Bordentown Trolley Company'.

The Great War did not bring electro-horticultural experimentation entirely to an end, but during the rest of the twentieth century it was fairly desultory. The British Board of Agriculture and Fisheries went so far as to set up an Electro-Culture Committee in 1918, which conducted a number of hopeful experiments before closing down, somewhat dejected, in 1936. The indefatigable American agricultural authority Liberty Hyde Bailey worked for years trying to establish the usefulness of electricity, accumulating data from some 50,000 plants and proving to his satisfaction that both lettuces and radishes could be helped. But on the whole too many trials proved fruitless, fertilizers often did the job better, and some 'experts' turned out to be fakes. Worst of all, occasional findings suggested that it might be better to avoid the whole sparky enterprise. When researchers at the Florida Agricultural Experiment Station ventured to see the effect of electrical current on 'Estes' rough lemon seedlings in 1975, they first found no effect. Then after a brief increase in growth, the issue was settled in a very final way. The trees died.

That may not, however, be the last word on the subject. In 2006 an English botanist named Andrew Goldsworthy came up with an ingenious explanation of why plants reacted positively to electrical current (if in fact they did). It was, it seems, a hereditary response to the atmospheric electricity produced by an approaching thunderstorm. Being zapped caused the plants to anticipate a good drink of water and prepared them for making use of it – and growing faster.

Frauds and Figments

The old story, most likely apocryphal, has it that a group of boys once decided to play a trick on the great Charles Darwin. They collected several sorts of beetles and other insects, carefully dismembered them, and glued the bits back together to create a new creature. Then they asked Darwin if he would identify their discovery. He contemplated it for a while and asked if had made a humming noise when it was alive. Indeed it had, sir, they replied. No question about it, then, Darwin said solemnly. It is a humbug.

I have a soft spot for this story; I've always been fond of hoaxes and frauds. Not because I'm any good at perpetrating them, of course (although I embarrassedly remember suffering one myself, when a photographer at the university daily paper I was editing managed to convince me that he'd found a way to develop film using Coca-Cola. I wrote an article about his achievement and was about to publish it, when he revealed all in the nick of time.) It's more matter of enjoying – and perhaps admiring – the ingenuity of the hoaxers. Fakery may be a slightly dubious art form, but it certainly demonstrates creativity, if of a slightly skewed variety.

Particularly in the field of botany, it is probably best to make a distinction between what's meant as a good-humoured jest and something more sinister. A few years ago, for example, a case of botanical hoaxing came to light that might well have done some serious damage in the world of scientific scholarship if it had gone unrevealed. (Ultimately it *did* do damage to the reputation of the perpetrator, although by the time he was conclusively found out he was dead.) It involved the purported discovery of certain otherwise uninteresting plants in a place where they simply didn't belong, but whose existence served to support a large if debateable theory about Ice Age survivals.

John Heslop Harrison already had a reputation for making extraordinary finds when in 1941 he announced that he had located a species of sedge, *Carex bicolor*, on the Hebridean island of Rum, hundreds of miles from any other sightings, and never seen before in Britain. As a distinguished professor of botany at Newcastle University, Heslop Harrison had to be taken seriously, and for many years was, but suspicions circulated in the highly competitive scientific community. Over the course of his career he had reported an improbable number of rare sedges in unlikely places. The *C. bicolor* brought the suspicions to a head. A Cambridge classicist named John Raven, not himself a botanist but deeply experienced in hunting wild plants, was able to establish that either the plants were not to be found where Heslop Harrison said they were, or worse, had quite obviously been planted there – 'dibbled in…more than half dead'. The fakery was obvious. Even so, it would be nearly fifty years – and long after his death – before the professor was unmasked. He was never challenged directly and Raven's damning report lay buried in a Cambridge library until the writer Karl Sabbagh unearthed it and resumed the investigation. Sabbagh's fascinating book *A Rum Affair* (1999) unravels the whole story, and goes some way towards showing how even the most respectable people can be drawn into committing fraud.

It was also well after John Gerard's death in 1611 that the author of *Gerard's Herball* was accused of botanical crime. There had already been complaints about mistakes in his book, including charges that he claimed to have found certain species in places where they simply didn't grow. Harder to swallow was his stubborn defence of the Barnacle Tree, 'one of the marvels of this land (we may say the World)' which supposedly grew in Scotland and the Orkneys and bore live geese. Most critical, however, was the attack by another botanist on Gerard's claims of native British origin for a number of imported plants, particularly the peony. 'The male Pieonie growth wild upon a conny berry [rabbit warren] in Betsome...in Kent', Gerard had declared firmly. Thomas Johnson not only didn't believe this, but reported having been told that Gerard himself had planted the peony – and then pretended to have found it 'by accident'. This seems entirely likely. Nobody else had ever found a peony growing wild in Kent before, or anywhere in Britain, for that matter, and Gerard was a recognized publicity hound.

Most botanical hoaxes have to do with reports of unlikely plants or plants growing in unlikely places; it's more difficult to assemble a convincing fake specimen. They do exist – the Museum of Garden History in London still has an example of the famous Vegetable Lamb or Borometz, the legendary plant/animal which from medieval times was believed to grow somewhere on the steppes of Central Asia. This particular specimen managed to fool a number of eighteenth century botanists until Sir Hans Sloan determined that it had actually been carved from the root of a fern.

As E. Charles Nelson has pointed out in an article on botanical hoaxes, researchers working with dried plants in a herbarium have been known to jumble fragments innocently and come up with what they thought was a new species. Deliberate frauds are relatively uncommon. One mentioned by Nelson is remarkable mainly because of the fame of the supposed perpetrator.

Auguste François Marie Glaziou (1828-1906) was a French landscape architect and botanist who spent much of his life in Brazil, where he designed many parks and gardens. His work at Quinta da Boa Vista, residence of the Brazilian royal family, made him particularly well-known. He also collected plants on a grand scale and is credited with discovering numerous new species; there is even a genus, *Neoglazovia*, named after him. Sometime in the 1880s he sent back to Europe a specimen of a bromeliad that Kew botanist J. G. Baker described – presumably hurriedly – and named *Quesnelia tillandsiodes*. In 1892, a picture of the new plant appeared in *Flora Brasiliensis*, whereupon a keen-eyed German bromeliad specialist pointed out that it was really a composite fake: flowers of a second bromeliad *Quesnelia liboniana* expertly inserted into the basal rosette of an entirely different genus (later suggested to be *Vriesea poenulata* – which Glaziou had also collected).

Just why Glaziou did this – as he surely did – remains a mystery. He had plenty of new plants to his name without needing a spurious one. But his tendency to cheat apparently ran deep. A later investigator studying his collections discovered several examples of tinkering, for example altering collection data on labels supplied by the original collector to make it appear that the plants had come from places as much as 2,000 miles away.

Perhaps this was meant to mislead follow-up collectors; in any case it added nothing to Glaziou's dented reputation for reliability.

There is equal mystery about the motive behind another bit of fakery described by Nelson. *Actinotinus sinensis* struck botanist Daniel Oliver at Kew as truly exceptional when he described it, named it, and published a picture of it in Kew's long-running *Icones Plantarum*. It had been sent from China in the 1880s by the plant collector and customs official Dr Augustine Henry, along with a great number of other specimens, many of them unfamiliar. Having done his duty by the new plant, however, Oliver realized that there was something a bit odd about it. He took a closer look, to discover that the flower of a viburnum had been 'artfully' inserted into the terminal bud of a Chinese horse chestnut (*Aesculus chinensis*). So much for *A. sinensis*. It was later learned that the villain was not Henry but his Chinese collector, who had in addition attempted to pass off two other chimæra: a viburnum flower stuck into a branch of sumac and a composition involving lespedeza. Neither of these got so far as naming or publication in the *Icones*. Nelson speculates that the collector was fed up with Henry, or possibly with collecting.

Creating an actual fraudulent specimen may be tricky and difficult, but there are easier ways to pull off a botanical hoax. If you aren't up to inventing a phoney plant, why not invent a phoney botanist? The most enterprising instance of this gambit is still being sorted out, nearly a century after it was first devised by an unknown prankster (or pranksters) in the pages of the large and impressively detailed *Cyclopedia of American Biography*. First published in six volumes between 1887 and 1889, and republished as recently as 1968, the *Cyclopedia* is still being consulted despite the fact that upwards of 200 of its entries have been shown to be entirely fictitious. Curiously, most of the fake biographies are of European scientists, largely botanists, who travelled to the Americas before the nineteenth century in search of plants or other new wonders. They are, I have to say, very convincing. Dates, titles of publications (in several languages), place names and so forth are all more than plausible. Appropriately, it was another botanist, John Hendley Barnhart of the New York Botanical Garden, who first spotted the fraud, unmasking fourteen of the ghostly explorers in an article published in 1919. Even then he suspected there were more fakes; their numbers have increased as sceptical investigators plumbed deeper to reveal further inventions. One after another – Lorenz Wenceslas Kerckhove, Eduard Sylvie, Giuseppe Igolino, Gustav Herman Kehr, Isidore Charles Sigismund Neé, and the rest – ceased their brief existence and passed into oblivion.

Could some of them have been real? Given the obscurity of many of the people covered and the way that the *Cyclopedia* was compiled, with a nameless crew of contributors being paid by the entry and little oversight, mistakes – if not fraud – was inevitable. But I am haunted by the idea that some poor Bavarian botanist, real enough but with modest achievements, might have been cast by accident into non-existence. One can be too cynical, after all. We have before us the case of *Impatiens psitticina*. A few years ago photographs of a beautiful but highly improbable flower circulated among plant collectors on the internet. Resembling a multicoloured flying parrot with a curved beak and apparently

Imaginary Plants

Three or four miles east of Junction 12 on the M4 Motorway west of London, in the middle of a modest forest on the north side of the road, a most peculiar conifer rises above the rest of the trees. Its branches go up when they should go down, and its trunk appears to be made of some kind of metal. Obviously it's not a tree but an imitation tree, and a pretty unconvincing one at that. No doubt some poor functionary sitting in an office at Orange or Vodafone decided that it would be less offensive to motorists and mobile phone addicts to fake a tree than erect a mast.

Inventing plants is not generally as tangible as this. In fact, most plants thought up from scratch remain distinctly imaginary, for obvious reasons. As Joyce Kilmer wisely observed, only God can make a tree. On the other hand, the world of imaginary botany has always been a richly populated one, and in recent times there has been a sort of surreal efflorescence.

Once upon a time, imaginary plants were not conceived of as imaginary at all. They may have been miraculous and improbable, but such specimens as the Vegetable Lamb or the Mandrake or the goose-bearing Barnacle Tree were presented in their day as perfectly real. The fact that nobody was able to produce an unchallengeable example was awkward, but irrelevant to the credulous; after all, these plants lived a long way off, and the best authorities were prepared to vouch for their existence. It would be a novelist named Ludwig Holberg, a science fiction writer before the genre existed, who came up with some of the first indisputably imaginary plants in his satirical *Niels Klim's Journey to the World Underground* (1741). In a plot resembling *Gulliver's Travels*, Holberg has Klim encountering an entire nation of ambulatory trees capable of talking – and of capturing and imprisoning poor Klim. (It is significant that the trees were hostile, at least in the first instance; a remarkable number of invented species tend to be bad news.)

In the eighteenth century the world of actual plants expanded vastly thanks to the discoveries of searchers in such places as the South Pacific, India, and the Americas. At that point nobody knew quite what to believe; strangeness came to be expected. For the sake of a good story, Nathaniel Hawthorne could invent an entire garden of poisonous plants in 'Rappaccini's Daughter'. But quite apart from the mere jokiness of Edward Lear's nonsense botany (which consisted mainly of an excuse for funny names like *Manypeeplia upsidedownica* for a plant with tiny humans hanging on a stem, or *Barkia howlaloudia* for dogs likewise), more speculative ideas tended to be stymied. How could mere imagination match the bizarre reality of some of the orchids being brought back from the South American rainforests, or the oddities from the Himalayas? We find the decadent writer Karl-Joris Huysmans, inspired by such discoveries, descending into a kind of vegetative insanity in his novel *A Rebours* (*Against the Grain*). His hero Des Esseintes, fascinated by corruption and artificiality, becomes obsessed by real plants that seem to imitate fake ones – *Sarracena* and *Cephalothus* that eat meat; '*Encephalartos horridus*, a gigantic iron rust-coloured artichoke'; 'the horrible streaked staining of the *Caladium* plants'.

But if Des Esseintes' nightmares were remarkable enough, they didn't satisfy writers like H. G. Wells. Wells may justifiably be called the father of imaginary plants in the modern sense, thanks to such ground-breaking fantasies as 'The Flowering of the Strange Orchid' (1894) and his novel *The First Men on the Moon* (1901). In the first, he devised an orchid that attacks its grower; while in the novel, along with some plausible science, he came up with an extra-terrestrial flora of huge fungi and sprouting lichens bearing a creepy likeness to true plants:

> And all that time the lunar plants were growing around us, higher and denser and more entangled, every moment thicker and taller, spiked plants, green cactus masses, fungi, fleshy and lichenous things, strangest radiate and sinuous shapes.

Not a pretty picture.

In the hands of science fiction writers, especially the earlier less-sophisticated ones, imaginary plants became a standard fixture, usually in the form of a handy frightener. Seldom do we find an agreeable or friendly artificial specimen. Typically, *The Devil Tree of El Dorado* (1897) by Frank Aubrey and Leigh Ellis features a tree with a taste for human flesh; threatening 'plant-men' of the kind originated by Edgar Rice Burroughs in *The Gods of Mars* (1918) subsequently turn up in dozens of pulp-mag stories. Probably the best-known of all the vicious vegetables appears in John Wyndham's horror novel *The Day of the Triffids* (1951), later a clunky film. Triffids, mysterious eight-foot-high insectivorous plants cultivated for their oil-bearing properties, suddenly take to walking about on short tripod legs, lashing out and poisoning humans with their whip-like sting. In the course of the book they pretty much take over the world (except of course for the hero and his girlfriend, who save it).

As science fiction becomes more complicated, imaginary plants appearing in it become more ingenious too. For example, there are the electrified Tesla Trees in Dan Simmons's Hyperion Cantos novels, which store up electricity inside their bodies and produce the fertilizer they need by releasing it all at once in a thunderous lightning bolt that burns away everything growing (or walking) nearby. In *Discworld* Terry Prachett invents the plants he calls 'reannuals', which because of 'an unusual four-dimensional twist in their genes', are normally planted a year *after* they are meant to bloom. The Vul Nut Vine, exceptionally, can flourish up to eight years before its seed is sown, and the wine made from its grapes confers the power of foresight.

When we come to *Harry Potter* and J. R. R. Tolkien's *Lord of the Rings*, whole beds of imaginary plants are on offer. Wikipedia devotes a dozen pages simply to listing them. Regrettably, however, few are truly clever or original, depending (in the case of *Potter*) on funny names – Abyssinian Shrivelfig, Gurdyroot, Screechsnap – or mere scene-setting, as with Tolkien's Ents or Pipe-weed. J. K. Rowling's Fanged Geranium has a certain classic appeal (it bites people) but the Bouncing Bulb, which refuses to be planted, is hardly memorable. Similarly, *Dungeons & Dragons* has a number of not-very-ingenious invented species. It might be necessary to conclude that the inspiration which brought so many wonderful fake plants into existence over the centuries had finally flagged. A couple of relatively recent publications, however, restore our faith.

The first, for which I confess a particular affection (I worked on the book as editor and greatly admired its author) is by the late Leo Lionni, a polymathic artist and writer whose work includes several highly acclaimed children's books. For some years he was art director of *Fortune* magazine. *Parallel Botany* is a deeply tongue-in-cheek volume masquerading as a legitimate scholarly study of a large array of invented flora, complete with footnotes, plausible but phoney authorities, plates and photographs. More than two dozen species and subspecies are described, with information on their discovery, habitats, history, morphology, characteristics, associated legends, and (in rare cases) food value. I am not exaggerating when I say that they are truly wonderful.

For example, there are the Tirils. This family includes both the *Tirillus mimeticus*, a plant so perfectly camouflaged 'that to all intents and purposes it is invisible' and the *Tirillus silvador*, a native of the western Cordilleras of Peru, which 'on clear nights in January and February' emits clear whistling sounds. *Anaclea taludensis* has the extraordinary property of appearing to remain the same size as one approaches it or goes further away. The *Artisia* group is oddly ambiguous; while almost certainly parallel, they 'often seem unbotanical, even nonorganic, and very likely of human origin', to the point where one researcher comments that it is not clear whether 'the plant expresses the influence of nature on art, or that of art on nature'. Thus *Artisia Arpii* closely resembles a collage by Jean Arp and *Artisia Calderii* a pendant by Alexander Calder – while (according to *Parallel Botany*) other forms of *Artisia* yet to be found may well anticipate the work of *all* artists. The Woodland Tweezers, being social plants, grow in groups that were inexplicable until a few years ago, when a Japanese researcher realized that they exactly reproduced the board position at the end of a famous game of *go* played many centuries ago by two legendary champions.

I'm tempted to go on talking about Lionni's imaginary plants, whose hysterical profundity come about as close as anything can to rivalling the unpredictable wonders of nature itself. It is pleasant to note that among them are no 'plant-men' or hostile fungi; *Parallel Botany* describes an entirely peaceable, if weird, kingdom. The same spirit, so far as I can see, animates a collection of self-styled 'cryptobotanists' who have recently published *A Field Guide to Surreal Botany,** consisting of descriptions of nearly 50 improbable plants. Some of them, admittedly, would hardly be welcome in your herbaceous border and some are more silly than clever, but anyone engaged by the idea of fantastic flora ought to enjoy reading about Dream Melons (*Melo somnio*) that 'play a vital role in the ecology of mirages in the Arabian desert' or Time Cactus (*Chronocactus hematophageis*). The latter, according to its discoverer, reproduces by means of a narrow wormhole extending from the time of germination at one end up to the present at the other, a concept as likely as anything else in modern physics (if not botany). The notion may not be up there with the Tiril, but it certainly beats flesh-eating trees.

---

* Edited by Janet Chui and Erik Jason Lundberg (Two Cranes Press)

ORIENTALIA

Japonaiserie

You don't just build a Japanese garden. Everyone knows that few styles of horticultural creation are so lapped about with formalities, precedents, rules, principles and prohibitions. After all, experts have been refining the appropriate concepts for something like a millennium or so, to the point where whole shelves of treatises offer guidance (or further confusion) to the perplexed landscaper worried about where to place that rock or plant that azalea. Consider the absolute elegance of such *chefs-d'oeuvres* as Kyoto's magnificent Ryōanji Garden, consisting of nothing but raked sand and a few rocks, or the moss and pruned trees of the Katsura Rikyū Detached Palace, or the miniature world of the tightly-enclosed Daiseinin, a few hundred square feet that brilliantly succeeds in suggesting infinity. The complexity is obvious, the details more than precise, the strangeness palpable, but at the same time gardens like these carry an extraordinary emotional charge. No wonder they made such an impact when reports about them first reached the West, and no wonder the first attempts to create Japanese gardens here went so awry. Later attempts too, for that matter.

From the start, misunderstandings went both ways. Not far from Ueno Park in Tokyo is a building that looks as though it escaped from some Gilded Age nightmare. Completed in 1896 in wood (which is made to look like stone), the Iwasaki Mansion has a *porte-cochere* surmounted by a square tower, vast windows, and a colonnaded veranda on the garden side described as being 'in the Ionian style of the Pennsylvania country house in the United States'. (If you find that hard to picture, I don't blame you. But it's a pretty impressive veranda.) It also boasts the first western-style toilet in Japan, together with iron radiators and some extraordinary wallpaper. Still, except as a testament to the muddled taste of the extremely wealthy in all ages (the money to build it came from the family that founded the giant Mitsubishi company) and the miracle of its survival through the vicissitudes of earthquake, fire, bombing and occupation by American forces after World War II, there appears to be nothing especially praiseworthy about the Iwasaki Mansion. The long, handsome Japanese-style dwelling attached to one corner of it in the rear is far more beautiful. The gardens, consisting as they do of little more than an expanse of grass surrounded by trees, with the odd stone lantern or statue lost in the shrubbery, are distinctly unmemorable. As a historical symbol, however, it commands respect. Its designer was Josiah Conder, an Englishman who not only led the way in bringing Western architecture and gardens to Japan but also played a central role in the fad for Japanese gardens in the West.

Conder was born in 1852 and trained in London with the famous medievalist architect William Burges. In 1877 he settled in Tokyo, not long after the restoration of the Emperor Meiji had ended hundreds of years of isolation and launched a national craze for modernization and all things Western. His timing was impeccable. Before long he was teaching a cohort of young Japanese architects who would themselves become important, and accepting commissions from bureaucrats, businesses and rich people for a wide range of buildings. His work included everything from the Bank of Japan to the National Museum to mansions and whole neighbourhoods – his red brick 'Londontown' development survived as a bit of Europe in the heart of Tokyo until the 1950s. In his history of Tokyo, Edward Seidensticker remarks that no other foreign architect who worked in Japan, even Frank Lloyd Wright, was as influential as Conder, or probably ever will be. His architectural influence, however, represents only a part of his importance.

Josiah Conder was only twenty-five when he arrived in Japan. It is plain that he was as ready to be seduced by things Japanese as his hosts were by things Western. He became fascinated by painting in the Oriental style, after some difficulty got a teacher (and a Japanese name, Akehide), and married a Japanese woman. (According to Seidensticker, he was good at fish.) He also discovered flower arranging and Japanese landscape gardening, both until then scarcely known and poorly understood in the West. In short, without ever losing his technical skills as a competent if not radically adventurous European architect, Conder apparently went native.

The first fruit of his Orientalist obsessions was a book called *The Flowers of Japan and the Art of Floral Arranging*, published in 1891. A serious piece of writing, beautifully produced in Tokyo and illustrated with woodcuts and line drawings by Japanese artists, *Flowers of Japan* showed that Conder had not only grasped the language but had gained a fairly sophisticated command of the aesthetics of Japanese floristry. Those inclined could follow its instructions to devise displays for moon viewing, old age celebrations, receipt of a promotion, or prayers for rain; suitable flowers for felicitous occasions were carefully spelled out, along with those species considered ominous or actually prohibited. To anyone for whom 'flower arranging' meant shoving a dozen roses in a vase, *The Flowers of Japan* must have looked frightening. It still does.

In 1893 Conder followed up with an even more impressive study, *Landscape Gardening in Japan*. Here, for the first time in English, was a detailed account of actual Japanese gardens, complete with dozens of extremely specific drawings – stones, ornaments, fences, pathways, bridges. Various types of stone lanterns were usefully categorised; plants, trees and shrubs recommended; whole ensembles described and illustrated with such clarity that – at least so it seemed – the most blundering European landscape designer could put together a convincing imitation. If anything, the how-to aspect of the book completely overwhelmed the philosophical; although Conder claimed to be offering 'an exposition of the rules and theories' behind Japanese garden art, the sort of thing he really told you was just how far apart your stepping stones should be, or why you needed a bronze crane for atmosphere. Worse, as the garden historian Loraine Kuck revealed many years later, his actual knowledge of Japanese gardens was narrowly limited to the relatively debased examples surviving in late nineteenth century Tokyo, and the handbooks of contemporary off-the-shelf professional garden builders. This left out of the picture nearly all of the magnificent earlier classic gardens, playing down the creative element and saddling the subject with a mass of often inappropriate rules.

Conder's books had an immediate impact among the gardening

cognoscenti in England and elsewhere in Europe, where there was plenty of enthusiasm for Japanese gardens combined with a muddle of inaccurate knowledge about them. The confusion could be traced back to mid-Victorian times. A few plant hunters, among them the professional collectors Robert Fortune and John Gould Veitch, had brought back a number of new species as early as the 1860s, and Fortune's haul included some *bonsai* trees. These miniatures particularly struck the fancy of certain avant garde horticulturists, who formed 'Japanese' gardens complete with small pagodas and stone lanterns around them. Then there was the rock garden craze sponsored by the plantsman-writer Reginald Farrer, which related to Japan largely because of the presence of stones; although in other respects there were few connections. Still another theme stemmed from the work of a diplomat stationed for a time in Tokyo. A. B. Freeman-Mitford (later Lord Redesdale) was enchanted by Japan, first by its culture (he published *Tales of Old Japan* in 1872) and then by its botany. Back in England, as owner of Batsford Park in Gloucestershire he created a personal version of a 'Japanese garden', one distinguished mainly by the presence of native Japanese plants such as conifers, maples, and bamboos. In no other respect did it resemble the real thing; in fact Freeman-Mitford, for all his admiration of Japanese culture, regarded the Japanese garden as 'a mere whimsical toy' full of 'symbols hard to understand'. His garden was basically an English-style arboretum with various Oriental statues planted amid the undergrowth. Still, his knowledge of bamboos was of another order – he put together a collection of fifty species and varieties and produced a splendid book describing them.

fragment of this garden survives to this day in London's White City, less than half a mile from my office in Shepherds Bush, right behind the BBC Television Centre (and a few yards from the Blue Peter Garden!).

The Japan-British Exhibition of 1910 in White City was projected as a trade fair intended to showcase Japanese exports. But another aim was to draw attention to Japan's richly mature culture. Gardens being a significant part of that culture, along with British enthusiasm for gardening generally, what could be more appropriate than to construct an example of the real thing? A committee was soon convened in Tokyo and experts assigned to design not one but two spacious gardens, a 'hillock' garden and a 'flat' garden. These categories were straight out of Conder, a connection possibly not accidental: one of the two designers, a painter named Kinkachiro Honda, had actually illustrated Conder's book. Like his fellow expert, Kenjiro Ozawa, he was a scholar of gardens but not a hands-on practitioner, and it is clear that the approach of both men was constrained in the same way Conder's had been.

The gardens were huge – the 'hillock' garden alone, known as The Garden of Peace, ran to more than two acres – and featured all the accoutrements the English visiting public would expect to find: pavilions, Buddhas, serpentine lakes, bridges, cranes and plenty of rock work. One unexpected feature was a vast painted canvas backdrop more than 30 feet high showing mountain scenery (White City proved to be very short of actual mountains). The 'flat' garden, The Garden of the Floating Island, had its own miniature artificial mountain and a waterfall nearly 20 feet high, along with a number of Japanese-style buildings. British visitors were reportedly pleased and admiring; the Japanese sponsors, including the Japanese ambassador, rather less so, complaining that the whole affair lacked subtlety.

Today, when you walk a block north along a quiet residential street from an unlovely stretch of the Uxbridge Road, you arrive at a small arched stone bridge crossing the arm of a reed-choked and unfortunately scummy pond. To your right, cloaked in azaleas and prostrate conifers, ledges of rock emerge from a low hillside; a modest cascade pours over and between them into the pond. It is a peaceful place, all that is left of the gardens built there a hundred years ago. Local people joined to clear and refurbish it a year or two ago, and the Japanese Embassy paid to replant it. Whether it is authentic or not is absolutely irrelevant.

From Chinese Gardens

Never underestimate the earning power of a green-fingered British nurseryman, or the acquisitiveness of a British gardener. In the mid-1750s James Gordon of the Mile End Nursery in London got his hands on 'a little stem and twig' of *Gardenia jasminoides* (now better known as *G. augusta*) from a collector/ botanist named Richard Warner. It was the first gardenia to reach Europe from China. Warner had received it a few years before from the captain of an East India Company ship, and had succeeded in flowering it. Gordon, however, did more. He set about propagating the plant from cuttings and layerings and by 1758, according to Jane Kilpatrick, was in a position to sell specimens for five or six guineas apiece (this at a time when a seaman on a China-bound ship earned twenty guineas *a year*). Within three years, even though the price had dropped by half, he had cleared £500 from his twig. Of course the gardenias, which none of his purchasers really understood how to cultivate, mostly died.

In a way, this series of events might be regarded as emblematic of the saga recounted in *Gifts from the Gardens of China.** The garden treasures – flowers, shrubs, trees – brought from China with considerable difficulty and many failures over the course of a hundred and fifty years were welcomed eagerly. They were – at least at first – rare and expensive. And more often than not they

---

* *Gifts from the Gardens of China: The Introduction of Traditional Chinese Garden Plants to Britain, 1698-1862.* By Jane Kilpatrick. (Frances Lincoln)

died, because the climate didn't suit or because the wrong sort of care was lavished on them. In time, however, such difficulties faded. The result, to be seen in virtually every garden today, is an array of plants so thoroughly integrated into our horticultural palette that it is hard to believe that we didn't always have them. The list is dazzling: chrysanthemums, bamboos, tree peonies, roses, pinks, Chinese asters, camellias, saxifrages, foliage plants, magnolias, campanulas, spirea, ornamental cherries, azealas, daphnes, viburnums, forsythia, wisteria, abelia, anemones – and many more.

Jane Kilpatrick tells the history of the introduction of these plants largely in terms of the men who found them and undertook to get them alive across the vast distance separating China from Europe, along with those other stalwarts who stayed home and devoted their energies to cultivating and naturalizing the new discoveries. There are a lot of plants and a lot of men, which to some extent excuses the dry nature of the prose; Ms. Kilpatrick will win no prizes for lively writing. But the quality of her research is first-rate and she clearly knows her plants as a skilled gardener. In addition to many familiar stories, she has dug out material on several fascinating and little-known lesser characters. For example there is Thomas Evans, a clerk in the East India Company Treasury Office, whose fascination with rare exotics apparently knew no bounds. In addition to collecting and growing a number of Chinese plants acquired through Company connections in Canton and sea captains, as well as supporting his own professional plant-hunter in the Far East, he may well have embezzled a considerable sum to support his hobby; the record is murky on the point. Nothing murky about his plant introductions, however, which included *Iris japonica, Begonia grandis* subsp. *evansiana,* the coralberry or spiceberry *Ardisia crenata, Rubus rosifolius* 'Coronarius' and Fan Grass (*Reineckia carnea*).

For most of the period covered by this book, collecting plants in China had little to do with scouring the countryside for rarities. Foreigners were kept firmly in their place, which was as a rule a very small and restricted place – mainly trading enclaves in Macao and Canton. Finding plants at all meant bribing native Chinese to bring them to you, or buying whatever was available in those few local nurseries collectors were allowed to visit. Some found it impossibly boring and took to drink. Yet even under these circumstances their achievements were remarkable.

If one had to pick a single species that most obsessed plantsmen looking to China for novelties, it would probably be the tree peony or mudan. Yearning began early – in 1653, a Jesuit priest living in China spoke of a '*Moutang,* a Flower called by them the King of Flowers. It's like a Rose but not prickly. It's white & purple & sometimes red & yellow'. But though it appeared on virtually every list of desiderata prepared for plant hunters, more than a century passed before a live specimen reached England. In 1787 Sir Joseph Banks, who was then in charge of the Royal Gardens at Kew, finally received a tree peony from his agent in Canton, only to have it expire immediately. The same thing happened again two years later. What no one understood – and was not to know for another sixty years, when the great plant hunter Robert Fortune learned about the practice – was that the tree peonies available in Canton were actually grown further north in a colder climate, dug up bare-root, and shipped south, where in the warmth of South China they quickly flowered, were displayed – and then died. There was in fact no more reason to think of them surviving than we would expect small potted azaleas or poinsettias forced for Christmas to survive.

Kilpatrick wisely ends her account in the middle of the nineteenth century, not because there were no more plants to discover in China – after all, yet to come were the vast unknown riches of southwest China – but because the principal handicaps of transport and distance had been lessened if not removed, and, with the opening of the whole country after the Opium War, the nature of the search had changed. Nathaniel Ward's fortuitous invention in 1829 of the sealed glass case for shipping living specimens made it far easier for them to survive the journey, while the time needed to make the trip had fallen from six months or more to two. In Europe, increasing knowledge and sophistication among gardeners meant that there were fewer of the familiar disasters attendant on ignorance – soaking plants that like to be dry, cosseting plants in the 'stove' that prefer to be outdoors. (The list of those initially overheated by mistake is impressive – camellias, wintersweet, *Chaenomeles speciosa*, *Magnolia denudata* and *M. liliiflora*, among others.) Moreover, with China itself no longer a sealed and impenetrable mystery, collectors could search for truly garden-worthy species in climates closer to that of Britain. But an incredible amount had already arrived. Early in the nineteenth century the landscape designer Humphry Repton could remark to a client 'there have been of late so many Chinese plants naturalized in England that it would not be difficult to enrich this spot with the productions of that country alone'. As we now know, there was more to come – and no doubt still is.

Pruning Japanese Style

I have always been a very nervous pruner. All the books say that you are supposed to be bold, that your shrubs and trees enjoy being handled vigorously, and that there's nothing more stimulating to the production of fruit and flowers than a sharp pair of secateurs (if not a saw). My reluctance is, however, profound. It stems from a deep-seated – if quite irrational – fear of doing damage to fragile plants, plus a certain degree of laziness. Consequently my apple trees look like hedgehogs, the plum is drooping overlong branches more or less to the ground, and most of the shrubs, whilst thriving, boast nothing but utterly natural shapes. I have, I hasten to say, managed to keep the wisteria under control (necessary in order to save the house), and likewise the hedges, but anyone wandering round the premises at Towerhill Cottage would quickly conclude that the pruning is, shall we say, underdone.

These thoughts arise because I have just returned from a trip to Japan, a place where pruning is king. I once believed that the main classical garden style in Japan was *karesansui*, the austere gravel and rocks of the Zen garden. While there are indeed plenty of splendid examples of this sort of 'horticulture' to be found in Japan, especially in the courtyards and precincts of famous old temples in Kyoto like Ryōanji and Ginkakuji, I now realize that the basic tool of the Japanese gardener is not the rake but the knife – or rather the pruning shears. What occupies him above all else is shaping his trees and shrubs – meticulously, endlessly, and with a connoisseur's eye for form.

And what forms! Visit, for example, the small, rather hard-to-find temple called Konpukuji, lost among the hills on the northeastern edge of Kyoto. There is a small expanse of raked white gravel, and indeed a very significant rock or two placed in it, but what you notice immediately are the wonderful blobs of smoothly sheared azaleas, like huge droplets of mercury, that seem to be gradually invading the gravel from the hill behind. There are several dozen of these, ranging in size from two or three yards across to a few feet, and they cluster together, rising up the hill beneath a few ancient yew pines (*Podocarpus macrophyllus*). The thatched roof of a 400-year-old tea house, buried in trees, crowns the slope.

Now each of these azaleas – called *karikomi* when so clipped, as I have learned from a handsome and informative book by Jake Hobson, *Niwaki* (Timber Press) – must be carefully shaped by hand, work that in this case, according to Hobson, is done by the sixty-year-old resident monk all by himself. It must take him most of year, whereupon it is time to start over. At Konpukuji, the azaleas are *Rhododendron obtusum*, an evergreen variety; other types – and other shapes, such as mountains or waves – are used elsewhere. A great deal of thought is put into the size and placement of *karikomi* (Hobson amusingly suggests arranging a selection of halved potatoes on a table to work out the proper effect before starting), and once they are mature (say a hundred years or so) equally great care is taken to keep them in their precise intended shape. Thus an old garden in Japan may be truly old, looking much as it did when it was first mature three or four centuries ago.

Karikomi, at least, are on the ground. Japanese gardeners are also prepared to go aloft, sometimes to considerable heights, to control the growth of larger trees. The old *Podocarpus* at Konpukuji, for example, has to be pruned once a year by an outside team. Just what this procedure can amount to was illustrated vividly to me one morning when we walked out of our inn in Nara to find a workman perched thirty feet up in a *Pinus thunbergii*. Scattered on the ground at the foot of the tree was a clutter of greenery, but no big branches. He seemed to be pruning the tree needle by needle.

Which is, in fact what he *was* doing. As it was autumn, this was the time for *momiage*, which involved thinning and pulling needles off new growth that had been encouraged a few months before by pinching out tip buds (candles). The fellow was still up there late in the afternoon when we returned, continuing to send down a light shower of pine needles for his assistant to sweep up. Fortunately the courtyard of the Kansaso contained only one big tree.

The point of all this, I learn from Hobson, is twofold: urging a young tree into a desired form, or maintaining the shape and size of a mature specimen. That may seem straightforward and familiar enough, but some of the shapes are anything but conventional. If Japanese gardeners are occasionally accused of a taste for artificiality or even grotesquery, one reason may be the violence tradition calls for inflicting on certain trees. Excluding for the moment *bonsai* (which I rather like although there are those who regard them as little more than tortured dwarves), consider some of the pruning styles described and illustrated by *Niwaki.* We find ways to make branches grow in zig-zags, or with trunks bending sinuously; for side branches to grow as a series of balls (*tamazukuri*) or as paired steps like so many plates jutting from the main stem; for converting natural branches into flat planes separated from each other, so that the whole tree resembles nothing so much as a Boy Scout practicing semaphore signaling. There is even a procedure called *monkaburi*, expressly designed to make a tree extend a branch over an entrance gate to produce a kind of natural archway. Broad-leaf evergreens – non-deciduous oaks, hollies, osmanthus and camellias – come in for other treatment. How about a *Quercus phillyreoides* shaped to look exactly like an eight-foot-high head of broccoli?

If this all sounds pretty awful, be assured that it isn't, in its place. Somehow or other, in the calm and elegance of a Japanese garden such aggressive pruning is absolutely appropriate and contributes essentially to the mood of controlled sophistication. Moreover, while a temple garden like Konpukuji or the neighbouring Shisendo will run off into the surrounding forest without any real boundary, there is a miraculously easy and satisfying transition between the intense intellectual artifice of the garden itself and the wildness beyond. The care with which the pruning is managed – along, of course, with other garden elements like water and gravel – plays an obvious part in this coherence.

But then care is a hallmark of the traditional Japanese gardener in every respect, to a degree quite shaming to this slap-dash Westerner. The smallest garden (and home gardens by necessity must often be very small, perhaps a tree and a few shrubs jammed into a courtyard or overlooked by a veranda) may well get the same

A Collector in the Right Place

'Good God! When I consider the melancholy fate of so many of [botany's] votaries I am tempted to ask whether men are in their right minds who so desperately risk life and everything else through their love of collecting plants'. So Linnaeus, the famous botanist who was himself a plant collector, mused when contemplating the daring if sometimes feckless activities of those who enriched our gardens. Still, clambering over mountains, sweltering in jungles, enmeshed in red tape in some remote consulate or bedecked with leeches, the great plant hunters not only found botanical treasures, for the most part they also found fame. From David Douglas (of the Douglas fir, and much else) to the Hookers, father and son, to Robert Fortune and Ernest Henry Wilson, the roll call of heroes echoes with glory.

Then there are those nobody has ever heard of, like George Rogers Hall.

It's not easy to find out much about Hall. He was born (in 1820) and spent much of his life in the town of Bristol, Rhode Island. Sadly but predictably, the list of notable inhabitants on Bristol's website, which includes a country and western singer and a professional golfer, totally ignores George Hall. Nor is there any mention of him among the 17,500 entries in the American Dictionary of National Biography. Even Wikipedia finds him unworthy of notice. Yet this is a man who introduced to the West not only that vastly important landscaping staple Japanese yew (*Taxus cuspidata*) and the star magnolia (*Magnolia stellata*), but dozens of other key species from cypresses to lilies to dogwoods. He did it, moreover, as an amateur.

Hall trained as a doctor at Harvard, graduating in 1846. It was a time when the Orient was much in the mind of young New Englanders, and Hall decided to try his luck in China. After practicing for a while in Shanghai, he joined with another Yankee to set up a small hospital catering to foreign sailors. The Seaman's Hospital had plenty of patients but Hall, now with a wife and three sons, sensed that he could do better in another line of work. With the Taiping Rebellion threatening to overrun China, the political situation looked grim. Sending his wife and children back to the States (one boy died en route), he took to trading in fine Chinese and Japanese art objects, buying up bronzes, ivory, jade and lacquer pieces. With two other young Americans, one of whom owned a schooner yacht, he sailed to a number of Far Eastern ports (suffering a run-in with pirates at least once, according to his grandson) in search of rare items. In 1855 he visited Japan, and eventually decided to settle there. Part of the appeal of Japan was the opportunity it presented for very profitable trade in gold and silver, and Hall was not a man to miss opportunities. He soon accumulated a considerable fortune.

But Japan, he found, had more than money to offer, and more to collect. Somewhere, perhaps at Harvard where the botanist Asa Gray was developing his theories about the curious relationship of species in places as widely separated as New England and Japan, or possibly during his childhood days on the family farm, Hall had formed a real and abiding love for plants. He instantly realized that Japan was full of unfamiliar varieties perfectly suited to temperate climates in America and Europe. Many had been described and named, especially by the German doctor-botanist Franz Balthasar von Siebold earlier in the nineteenth century, and in some cases foreign herbaria boasted dried examples. But relatively few living specimens of any of them had yet reached gardens abroad. After all, the journey was immensely long, and until the invention of the glazed, sealed Wardian box there was no practical way to keep plants alive over the whole distance.

When Hall settled in Yokohama, Japan – after centuries of isolation – had been open to the outside world for less than a year. Only a few Europeans had been able to study its flora first-hand. Now hundreds of trees, shrubs and herbaceous species native to the country but unknown in America and Europe were available for the collecting. And collectors came: the aging Von Siebold (who had been expelled thirty years earlier) turned up; so did the Scottish plant hunter Robert Fortune, who had been scavenging in China. John Gould Veitch of the Veitch nursery dynasty came collecting, along with the Russian botanist Carl Maximowicz. Hall fortuitously found himself in an extraordinarily lucky position for someone knowledgeable about plants.

He promptly began building a garden. It must have been a fairly jumbled affair, designed less for beauty than capaciousness, but it soon contained a remarkable group of plants. Von Siebold helped out by presenting Hall with some unusual varieties; Fortune, passing through in 1860, made use of the garden as a sort of horticultural warehouse for his own collections until they could be packed up for shipment. (As it happened, Fortune and Veitch were competitors, working for different principals. Neither won the race to get their new plants back to England because their crates ended up on the same ship.)

In 1861, Hall sent his first shipment of plants, mostly trees, back to America. A friend agreed to tend them during the three-and-a-half month voyage. Their destination was the estate of a prominent Bostonian named Francis Lee, but within months of their arrival Lee (soon to be a colonel) was swept up in recruiting a regiment of volunteers for the Union Army in the Civil War. Hall's precious cargo – *Cornus kousa, Wisteria floribunda,* hiba arborvitaes, a variegated gingko, umbrella pines and more – might have been orphaned except for the intervention of an improbable saviour: Francis Parkman, the testy, near-blind, near-crippled historian of the American West, author of *The Oregon Trail* and numerous other classic works, who had developed a great interest in gardening after his health began to fail. Parkman specialized in roses, but he was happy to get Hall's collection.

Among the more remarkable items in Hall's shipment were bulbs of the magnificent *Lilium auratum,* the goldband lily. Parkman soon showed himself to be a worthy recipient by flowering it for the first time outside Japan. Because he waited to exhibit the bloom at a meeting of the Massachusetts Horticultural Society, he missed out on the privilege of naming it by a matter of days; Veitch had also sent bulbs from Japan and the flower was shown in London, where John Lindley promptly described and named it. Parkman, however, subsequently used the goldband to breed some spectacular cultivars, notably the *Lilium parkmanni,* which he eventually sold to an English grower for a thousand pounds.

There was more in Hall's first shipment – one particularly attractive item, a crabapple with semi-double blossoms would claim both his name and that of Parkman (*Malus halliana* Koehne var. *parkmannii*). But it was his second shipment in 1862, that really established his importance. This time, Hall himself shepherded the cases on the long voyage across the Pacific, taking them to the Samuel Parsons Nursery in Flushing, Long Island for propagation. Before long trees, shrubs and flowers from this treasure trove were growing in gardens all over the Eastern United States – and still are.

According to a list compiled in the 1920s by Hall's grandson, the plants handed over to Parsons added up to some fifty or sixty species, many introduced alive for the first time outside Japan. Some are real prizes, notably the star magnolia and the Japanese yew. Half a dozen Japanese maples, several kinds of Japanese wisteria, 'ten garden forms' of sawara cypress (*Chamecyparis pisifera*), the hinoki cypress (*Chamaecyparis* obtusa), lilies, chrysanthemums, more seeds of the umbrella pine, the Japanese zelkova (*Zelkova serrata*) and many more reached the delighted nurseryman. A letter published in a contemporary horticultural magazine and quoted by Stephen Spongberg in his fine book *A Reunion of Trees* suggests the excitement of the moment:

> If you have ever seen the eagerness with which a connoisseur in pictures superintends the unpacking of some gems of art, among which he thinks he may possibly find an original of Raphael or Murillo, you will have some idea of the interest with which all, both employers and

propagators, surrounded those cases when they were being opened.

The excitement was justified.

When Hall returned from Japan, he moved to North Farm, the family place in Rhode Island, where he planted some of his oriental trees and shrubs. But he wasn't the sort to settle down. In 1865, at the end of the Civil War, he went south, first to Georgia (where as an alien Yankee he had an uncomfortable time of it) and then to Florida. For many years he moved back and forth between Florida and New England, but then made the mistake of so many entrepreneurs intoxicated with the idea of Floridian property. With several associates he put money into building a couple of hotels and some cottages on the Atlantic Coast south of Jacksonville. The enterprise ran successfully for a few years but then a major supporter pulled out, one hotel burned to the ground just as the insurance lapsed, and a storm destroyed the other hotel, bankrupting Hall. As his grandson observes, he had 'little judgement' about financial matters. To put a cap on things, an investment in a gold mine went bad and the Great Freeze of 1881-82 wiped out his remaining asset, an orange grove. For the rest of his life he eked out a living by selling off Japanese and Chinese antiquities he had brought back from the Far East.

Some remnants of Hall's plantings in Rhode Island and in Florida survived for a long time, and perhaps still do. In the 1920s, when his grandson wrote his memoir, a huge spreading Japanese yew thrived in Bristol, along with a loquat, a Japanese walnut (*Juglans seiboldiana*), a hardy orange (*Poncirus trifoliate*), a big zelkova, pines and cypresses, and a number of other trees, though not necessarily the original specimens. In Florida he found a big magnolia, but not much else. In the 1980s, the yew (then 30 feet tall and 130 feet in circumference), a hinoki cypress, and the zelkova could still be seen growing at North Farm.

It must be noted that Hall was also responsible for a somewhat less happy plant introduction, one which, if relatively scarce in Rhode Island (the winters tend to be too cold) has turned out to be a pest and a plague over vast expanses of the East and the Midwest. *Lonicera japonica* 'Halliana', Hall's honeysuckle, a vigorous and moderately attractive ornamental climber, arrived as part of the Parsons shipment and for thirty years or so behaved itself. Then it escaped, presumably with the help of birds that ate its firm black berries and spread the seeds. Its true nature was revealed. Thanks to its twining growth habit and sheer energy (it can grow fifteen meters in a year and send roots a metres deep) it went on to strangle thousands of acres of native saplings and small trees. *Gray's Manual of Botany*, not mincing words, called it 'a most pernicious and dangerous weed'. A pity that of all the plants introduced by George Rogers Hall it is by far the best-known – and almost the only one – to bear his name.

GARDEN TOURS

H. Avray Tipping and a Debate Reconciled

'Many', wrote William Robinson with his customary asperity, 'not satisfied with the good word "Landscape Gardener"…call themselves "Landscape Architects", a stupid term of French origin implying the union of two absolutely distinct studies'. The great spokesman for natural gardening made no secret of his disdain for architects, landscape or otherwise, especially those who fancied themselves omnicompetent. An architect could help the gardener by building a beautiful house – 'that is his work' – but ought to go no further. A garden was a gardener's business.

While there is no reason to think that Robinson did not mean what he said, it has to be admitted that he spoke in the heat of battle. The Great Debate – or, if you prefer, the frustrating argument – between his followers and their opponents, represented principally by the architect Reginald Blomfield, author of *The Formal Garden in England*, was raging in the 1890s, at a time when the Victorian tradition of spot planting and bedding out was coming to a little-lamented end. The Edwardian era was at hand, and Robinson was convinced that his approach – relatively unconstrained, with natural forms, plenty of flowers (preferably native), richly unpredictable climbers and ramblers, the whole glorious panoply of nature itself focused and enhanced – represented the future for British gardening. Blomfield, in an equally polemical mode, argued for what he called 'formality', which was really a sort of throwback version of the early seventeenth century English style, integrating house and 'old-fashioned' garden with hedges, topiary, walls and turf. He evoked his ideal in typically romantic prose:

> Behind the lawyer's house, with its white sash-windows and delicate brick work, there may still survive some delightful garden bright with old-fashioned flowers against the red brick wall, and a broad stretch of velvety turf set off by ample paths of gravel, and at one corner perhaps, a dainty summerhouse of brick, with marbled floor and panelled sides; and all so quiet and sober, stamped with a refinement that was once traditional, but now seems a special gift of heaven.

In retrospect, it is odd that so much of Robinson's invective fell on the heads of architects. There may have been a touch of class envy involved – being a self-made man, Robinson particularly execrated the grand country houses like Alton Towers and Shrubland Park built by Victorian oligarchs. Blomfield actually had no brief for them either. He liked carpet bedding as little as Robinson did, or empty grandiosity. Nor was he an especially distinguished architect. What he did stand for was a sensible combination of house and garden into a sort of emotional ensemble. It was a reflection of the thinking (and doing) of contemporaries like William Morris and the Arts and Crafts School, and it proved to be deeply attractive. Given the intense, almost universal, involvement of architects in most of the great gardens to be built in Britain during the first decades of the twentieth century, one would have to say that if Blomfield didn't win the debate, he didn't lose it, either.

Certainly I find it easy to like the architectural approach, especially as it is shown in the delightful drawings by H. Inigo Thomas that illustrate Blomfield's book. Because of their scale – many of the 'formal' gardens tend to be small – and their focus, with easily comprehended elements like enclosures and steps, they can be more appealing and less intimidating than some of Robinson's more adventurous recommendations, forward-looking as they might be. When in 1954 Geoffrey Jellicoe praised Robinson as 'the basis of the modern way of thought' in landscape design, and remarked that Blomfield 'has passed out of history', he may have been technically accurate – the tide of fashion was flowing in Robinson's direction – but in fact the opposition between the two men was never real. Gertrude Jekyll famously observed that both were wrong, and both right.

Just what she meant by this gnomic statement is itself open to debate. So far as I'm concerned the answer lies in the sort of gardens that were created in the wake of Robinson and Blomfield – and Jekyll herself – which happen to be among our most pleasing. I don't speak now of great gardens like Hidcote (though that surely qualifies as a delight and a model), but of the work of such minor masters as H. Avray Tipping, whose sun of fame has pretty well set, though several of his gardens survive not far from where I live in Monmouthshire. As illustrations of the way architecture and horticulture – Robinsonian and otherwise – can and should be reconciled, they are exemplary.

Tipping was not himself an architect, but he had a certain amount of architectural training and became the country's leading authority on old houses. Born into a prosperous middle-class family in 1855, after leaving Oxford he began by buying and selling a series of small and medium-sized estates, rebuilding and restoring where necessary, and surrounding them with new or refurbished gardens. He put in water features, redirecting streams or, where necessary, installing pumps. When all was done to his satisfaction, he moved on, presumably making a bit of money in the process. In 1911 money ceased to be any kind of a problem when he inherited £200,000 (worth perhaps £17 million in purchasing power today).

As Tipping gained expertise as a gardener, he began writing pieces for William Robinson's magazine *The Garden*, and when that magazine was taken over by *Country Life* went on to produce a long series of detailed and learned articles on country houses. So definitive and popular were these that the magazine itself changed its nature, leaving behind its original format as a sporting journal dealing mainly with hunting, racing and shooting. Tipping also turned out volumes on English furniture, the wood sculptor Grinling Gibbons, the Welsh Fusiliers and several books on English gardens and gardening. Meanwhile, he embarked on still greater building and horticultural enterprises.

In 1894, he bought the ruins of Mathern Palace in the Monmouthshire lowlands west of Chepstow, all that was left of the residence of the Bishops of Llandaff from 1406 to 1706. Pulling down what he had to and using the materials to reconstruct the rest, he rebuilt the medieval palace with admirable historical accuracy, and lived there for a number of years. The gardens he built from scratch – extensive lawns, terraces, flagged paths, water gardens and fish ponds, with yew hedges (complete with topiary foxes, cocks and pheasants) and limestone walls providing structure. Then, with his inheritance in hand, in 1912 he started work on a house of his own at Mounton, a village near Chepstow. This was a serious undertaking that eventually cost him £40,000. In a rocky sandstone gorge he built a water garden, and then installed a steam pump to carry water to the mansion at the top of the adjoining hill. The gardens, like those at Mathern, were exuberantly floral, designed to supply masses of colour in every season. Not for nothing was Tipping a friend and disciple of Gertrude Jekyll. But they were also determinedly architectural, with a broad flagged terrace, a walled rose garden, parterres and pergola. Twelve gardeners were required to keep it in order.

Possibly overcome by the grandness of it all, or simply following his usual practice of moving on impatiently when a house and garden was finished, in 1922 Tipping made over Mounton to a relative and proceeded to build yet another house, at the top of a steep wooded ridge near Monmouth. High Glanau, as he named it, is domestic, more modest in scale than Mounton but almost perfect in the way it integrates house and grounds – including, as a splendid bonus, a spectacular view down and across the broad Usk Valley to the Black Mountains. Thanks to the efforts of the present owners, Helena Gerrish (who has become an expert on Tipping) and her husband, the whole ensemble is gradually being brought back in line with its original infinitely engaging conception. (Not a simple undertaking: it included removing a full-size in-ground swimming pool that a previous owner had dug into the middle of a parterre terrace.)

And what was this conception? In 1929 Tipping wrote two

lavishly illustrated *Country Life* articles about High Glanau, and in them talks about his philosophy of garden design. He had of course lived through the Robinson-Blomfeld contretemps and, like Gertrude Jekyll, decided that the proper approach lay somewhere between the two contenders. 'The rival schools were not merely accepted', he writes, 'but fused, and the happy coalition that arose and still prevails combines knowledge of architectural treatment with comprehension of cultural needs, of botanical resource and of natural effects'. This may seem obvious, but at High Glanau Tipping undertook to give physical reality to it.

The house is low and compact, with numerous gables beneath sweeping roofs in the Arts and Crafts style. It sits comfortably in one of the few places on the steep hillside where there is a bit of flat land; immediately in front, just beyond a flagstone terrace, a flight of steps plunges down to an octagonal pool with a fountain, beyond which the woodland begins, cut back discreetly to reveal the view. To the left of the house Tipping created terraces flanked by walls and hedges against the savage southwest wind, making possible several borders more than a hundred feet long, full of perennials and bulbs. (*Lonicera nitida* formed one of the hedges, one of the earliest such in Britain. Presumably he employed an ever-ready clipping staff.) Tipping's aim, as he put it, was for the 'house border and terrace bed [to] carry the dwelling feeling into the open and provide immediate floral colour and decoration as you step out'. It does this triumphantly. In all, the gardens surrounding the house, like the house itself, display an unpretentious warmth and sense of control, architectural but consistent with the needs of the plants that compose it.

There is more to the gardens at High Glanau (they cover 12 acres); beyond his Blomfieldian 'geometrical gardening', Tipping made extensive plantings in the woodland both above and below the house. Today, much of this is still in the process of being restored but it is already possible (especially with the help of the *Country Life* articles) to see what he was aiming at. It might be called Robinsonian – meandering walkways planted with rhododendrons, hydrangeas, phlox and astilbes, sets of rough stone steps and paths, a fern dell. Tipping himself refused to call it 'wild', arguing that 'nurture and kemptness' are 'the essence of gardening', and 'there is nothing really wild at Glanau. There are woodlands more or less treated, more or less left to native vegetation, more or less swept and garnished. It is gardening, but with nature kept in the forefront of set purpose'.

So High Glanau is a compromise, one which takes into account the need for formality at the same time as it takes advantage of the drama of the location. In his other landscape designs (notably at Wyndcliffe, another Monmouthshire Arts and Crafts mansion) Tipping shows the same balance. As a gardener I'm drawn to the formality – clipping that lonicera may be intimidating, but nothing compared to maintaining woodland in a semblance of a garden – yet one has to be grateful that no aspect of the natural setting or the potential of horticulture has been slighted. Flowers are wonderful but so are walls; how nice to have both!

Piercefield and the Picturesque

If you leave your car in the car park at the Chepstow Leisure Centre and make your way downhill past the tennis courts and the football pitch, you come to a fence (easily climbed) separating you from a clearly marked and reasonably well-used path. Take the path. There are wet leaves underfoot, and beechnuts as closely packed as gravel, and in the distance rooks are swooping and cawing. Otherwise it is quiet. The path goes through scrub woods broken occasionally by enormous old trees – beech, oak, a few chestnuts, yews so tangled after falling and growing up again that you can hardly make out their original trunks. Though you can sense that you are walking along a steep slope, for most of the way there are no views, or almost none, because the foliage is too dense. At one point, the path opens out above a precipice; here you can see Chepstow Castle in the distance, and rock cliffs on the far side of the Wye. There is even a battered and decaying bench on which in better days one might have rested while gazing. Further on, a few more openings yield views to the river. But on the whole it is a pleasant woodland walk, nothing more.

In fact, this whole hillside, which belongs to the now derelict estate called Piercefield, is a testament to the power of vegetal exuberance. A couple of centuries ago, presumably less comprehensively wooded, the walks located here were famously a place of pilgrimage for landscape connoisseurs, the much-visited climax of the most fashionable aesthetic experience of the late eighteenth century – the Great Wye Tour.

In its forty miles between Ross and Chepstow, where it finally flows into the Severn Estuary, the River Wye winds through spectacular scenery. Riverside pastures harbour sheep and cattle, the tree-clad hills behind grow steeper and cling more tightly to the river until bare rock cliffs emerge. Midway, the standing ruins of Tintern Abbey offer romantic perfection. Hardly surprising, therefore, that the apostle of the Picturesque, William Gilpin, chose to make this the subject of his first book, *Observations on the River Wye*, which he published in 1782. Gilpin was not the first tastemaker to discover the Wye, of course – Tintern already had a reputation as a 'romantick' pile – but he was in the vanguard of the move toward the appreciation of natural beauties and his writings were enormously influential. Gilpin's own take on the 'picturesque' was straightforward if a bit simple-minded, defining it as something that would make a good picture, i.e. a picture by Claude or Poussin or Salvator Rosa. And if this meant proceeding by way of judgments that we today would regard as a bit weird (a cow, he declared, is the most picturesque animal, although a sheep is agreeable too, unless sheared) it was a philosophy that could be readily grasped by anybody, even tourists. It fitted into, and encouraged, the burgeoning enthusiasm for the Romantic movement in the all the arts, from gardening to poetry. Soon no one of discrimination was likely to turn down a chance to savour the beauties of the Wye. By the 1790s it was the most popular British tour destination.

While most of the fascination of the Wye Tour lay in its

natural wonders – the hills, the ruins, the placid river Alexander Pope termed 'pleas'd Vaga' – the Piercefield walks were different. They were deliberately planned and built as an essay in the Picturesque, in effect appropriating an entire landscape in the service of dramatic and aesthetic experience. In 1740 Colonel Valentine Morris, a military man enriched by West Indian estates, bought Piercefield and on his death a few years later passed it on to his son, also Valentine. Settling there in 1752, and possibly inspired by his wife, whose brother-in-law owned the famous gardens of Nun Appleton in Yorkshire (the subject of Andrew Marvell's wonderful poem), Morris set about creating a park in the grand style. Its principal – and most original – feature was not the sweeping lawns and well-placed copses decreed by such as 'Capability' Brown, but a skein of graded pathways and steps through the woodland along the cliffs overlooking the river. These were by no means random – on the contrary, each was carefully placed to maximize a visitor's sense of surprise, with vistas suddenly opening out or unexpected arrivals at the edge of a precipice. Terrifying heights, ruins intended to inspire romantic associations, vast panoramas – all were on offer. There was a grotto carved into the rock and studded with 'stones of various kinds; copper and iron cinders, etc.'; a 'Druid's Temple'; a 'Chinese seat' and various other resting spots with views. Above another cavern chopped out of the rock Morris placed the statue of a giant carrying a huge stone; this soon fell victim to the weather, with the stone, and then the giant himself, toppling down the cliff to be seen no more. Nearby, a small cannon could be fired to create echoes. A long zigzag set of steps led from the river to join the paths, thus making access possible for tourists, who generally came down the river from Ross by boat. The whole ensemble came to be known as the Piercefield Walks.

As Elizabeth Whittle's excellent account of Piercefield makes clear, Morris's walks immediately became extremely popular among those in search of picturesque beauties. John Byng, later Viscount Torrington, was moved to write a poem about the Grotto, observing that the prospects 'afford[ed] every charm of rock, wood and water'. Coleridge, thoroughly awed by the views, wrote 'Oh what a godly scene…The whole world seemed imaged in its vast circumference'. Arthur Young declared that in one spot there was a view 'at the very idea of which, my pen drops from my hand: – the eyes of your imagination are not keen enough to take in this point, which the united talents of a *Claud*, and a *Poussin*, would scarcely be able to sketch'. For his part Gilpin, while praising 'all these inchanting scenes', complained about some of the shrubberies Morris had introduced as 'injur[ing] the grandeur, and simplicity of the whole'. He also complained about the 'sludgy shores' at the foot of the cliffs, because the Wye at this point is tidal. In view of Morris's extraordinary exertions these might be considered ungracious comments. On one occasion, while planning a perspective, he is said to have fallen off the Lover's Leap, a viewpoint 180 feet above the river, and was saved only by grabbing some bushes on the way down.

Valentine Morris was rightly proud of his creation, which seems to have been finished by 1760. For the next decade or so he was always ready to supply visitors with guides 'to conduct them everywhere, and not one of them is suffered to take a farthing'.

But by the 1780s the walks were being neglected. Byng noted that they were 'ill kept, some of them...almost impassable', which may have reflected the difficulties Morris found himself in. He was a gambler and a poor businessman; he had spent lavishly on his property; and he also made the mistake of getting into politics, which in the eighteenth century could be a very expensive business. In 1784 he sold up and sailed off to the West Indies. (His fortunes did not improve there: although he became governor of St. Vincent, the island fell to the French and Morris was bankrupted. He returned to London and debtor's prison, dying in 1789.) The purchaser of Piercefield, a banker named George Smith, engaged a young architect, later the famous Sir John Soane, to prepare drawings for an elegant neo-classic mansion on the hill above. He also undertook to refurbish the walks, realigning some of them and adding new features to improve Morris's effects. But then Smith's bank failed, and even before the house was completed he too had to sell.

And so it went. Smith's successor finished the house before moving on. Another West Indian sugar heir – extraordinarily, the son of an English planter and a black slave – took it over, extending the property as a whole to some 3,000 acres in the course of the fifty years he occupied it. Tourists drawn to the Wye by such powerful works as Wordsworth's 'Lines Written a Few Miles above Tintern Abbey' still came to visit, but in smaller numbers; owners less open-handed than Morris had been (he reportedly suffered having his fruit trees and conservatories 'stripped for the refreshment of those who came continually to enjoy the luxuries of his favourite spot') started finding them a nuisance. For a while

Smith allowed the public to enter on Tuesdays and Fridays. Then privacy gradually became more important. Moreover, tastes were changing and the picturesque was no longer the latest thing. As careful maintenance ceased many of the views filled in and some of the paths began to be slippery and dangerous. By the 1850s, according to Whittle, the whole system was closed to the public and fell into disuse. The house and park remained – indeed it was grand enough to be (unsuccessfully) proposed in 1856 as a residence for the Prince of Wales. The early twentieth century saw an extraordinary episode below the Piercefield cliffs when an American doctor named Orville Owen, convinced that Francis Bacon was the true author of Shakespeare's plays, concluded that Bacon had secretly buried manuscripts there. Owen dug many holes but found nothing.

Today the Piercefield estate, or what is left of it, belongs to Chepstow Racecourse Ltd., whose track occupies a large part of the grounds. A cross-country course, grazed by sheep, lies across the broad sloping meadows in front of the house. Piercefield House is a hollow shell, an enormous stately roofless structure with trees growing in it and crumbling lintels. For more than seventy-five years it has been empty, increasingly derelict. Rumour has it that it was used for artillery practice during the war. Yet recently architects prepared drawings showing how it might be restored and the estate agents Jackson-Stops are advertising it for sale for £2 million, presenting someone else (with West Indian sugar money?) with the opportunity to 'recreate a classic country estate' in 'one of the most outstanding, Picturesque and sublime landscapes of eighteenth century Britain'. It's a challenge: at the moment even approaching the place is too dangerous to attempt for fear of falling masonry. The £2 million gets

A Visit to Highgrove

Ordinary people don't get invited to Highgrove much. Like most things connected with British royals the place is extremely private. As the home of the Prince of Wales and his wife the Duchess of Cornwall, it is where he has spent twenty six muddy years creating what must be the finest garden anywhere based on strict organic principles, and you either need to be special, or to wait at least three years after applying, to have a hope of breaching the gates.

But Prince Charles is also an author, which basically explains why a handful of American journalists were offered a tour the other day. I was delighted to join in, not least because there was a chance I'd learn what to do about my potato blight. I'm an organic gardener too, though less by conviction than lassitude, because I make compost but never get round to using pesticides.

Charles's book, *The Elements of Organic Gardening* (largely written by Stephanie Donaldson), sets forth his horticultural philosophy and buttresses it with a great many splendid colour photographs, many of them featuring HRH and Camilla and/or spade. On the whole the book brilliantly supports the argument for going organic – no pesticides or chemical fertilizers, an abiding respect for natural processes, compost, and horse manure – but to be honest it's nothing compared to the argument put forth by Highgrove itself.

The day I went there it was threatening rain (no small matter in this corner of England – the floods that swamped the Severn Valley two weeks ago were still draining away) but Highgrove had clearly not suffered from the wet summer. Everything was lush, even more spectacular than usual. There were some problems, of course – the 4 ½-acre wildflower meadow, normally cut in July, was still a sea of long grass, while the slug population seemed happier than ever.

David Howard, the head gardener, a husky 49-year-old with a well-tailored moustache, a Roman haircut and an amiably knowledgeable manner, showed us around in Charles's absence. (If Charles hadn't been absent, in Scotland for August, we wouldn't have been there anyway – no outsiders allowed when the royal couple is in residence.) Howard, however, is clearly the man to talk about the gardens. He has been at Highgrove for nine years, and during this time many of the principal developments have taken place. Much as he stressed that the Prince was the man who made the decisions, Howard himself seemed to be personally acquainted with every tree, plant and topiary snail. And there are plenty.

Highgrove is actually a 15-acre series of separate gardens more or less surrounding a small, handsome, balustraded manor house built in the 1790s. Eight full-time gardeners work under the head gardener, which may seem like a lot until you grasp the amount of labour involved. The topiary alone, which involves dozens of shapes carved in box and yew not only stretching down a long alley behind the house, but also scattered elsewhere – cones, spirals, mushrooms, even Platonic and Archimedean geometrical solids ordered by the Prince – must require hundreds of hours of clipping. Then there is the orchard, the Arboretum, the huge one-acre Walled Garden filled with vegetables, herbs and flowers, the Stumpery and Woodland Garden featuring ferns (including tree ferns from the Antipodes), and more. Such small exquisite enclosures as the Sundial Garden beside the house, planted by David Howard with black and white perennials chosen to bloom sequentially for ten months of the year, or the Azalea Walk, with its underplanting of bulbs and season-extending clematis, simply cannot take care of themselves. To look as they do, clear of weeds and invaded by only those self-seeders you really want, demands enormous amounts of attention. Even the Wildflower Meadow needs replanting with 500 camassia bulbs a year.

Given the health and vigour of the plants at Highgrove, it is sometimes hard to grasp that no artificial fertilizers or pesticides are used. Even the hostas – which are royal favourites and abound throughout the grounds – show only minor evidence of slug damage. I find this inexplicable, judging from my own experience, but Howard claims that natural predators like birds and hedgehogs will keep the pests in check, if you let them. I really want to believe him.

'Organic' is never out of the picture at Highgrove. Signs reading 'BEWARE, YOU ARE NOW ENTERING AN OLD-FASHIONED ESTABLISHMENT' and 'THIS IS A GMO [genetically modified organism] FREE ZONE' are the first things you see upon arriving. Prince Charles has developed quite a reputation for a sort of natural conservatism, and Highgrove is deliberately designed to illustrate the way it works in practice. Thus the emphasis on avoiding pollution and waste, which extends even to recycling water by use of a reed bed purifying system, and of course avoiding anything that smacks of genetic engineering (horrors). If the press in Britain has not always been either sympathetic or kind to him (complaining, for example, about the amount of money spent on the gardens and other princely hobbies, although at the same time most of his business enterprises are hugely profitable), the American media, Howard notes, are kinder.

The real organic purist might be taken aback at the amount of machinery needed to keep the gardens in order. Tractors, lawnmowers of varying sizes, chippers to deal with the woody slash, diggers and tippers. The compost heaps, things of beauty to both David Howard and, enviously, me, are turned weekly using a mechanical bucket, which makes possible the production of black, fragrant compost containing 3.5% nitrogen in six weeks or so – at a rate of no less than ten tons a year. (Howard's formula, for those who care, calls for equal parts of straw and grass clippings. No leaves.) In what may be an apology for all this internal combustion, the Wildflower Meadow is mowed and raked with a team of Suffolk Punch horses.

Anybody who manages to get into Highgrove is bound to be struck by the beauty of the place. Beyond that, there's no denying that it presents a brilliant case for organic gardening, or least gardening in a more sensible and natural way. I wish I could report that I learned what to do about my potato blight, but all David Howard could suggest was what I've already done – chop off all the tops at the first sign, dig the potatoes, and trust to God.

Royal Gardeners

Versailles has never been the object of universal admiration. Horace Walpole called it 'a garden for a great child'. The waspish Duke Saint-Simon, notably unfriendly toward Louis XIV, founder and proprietor of this vast assemblage of fountains, allées, palaces, lakes, statuary and assorted horticultural splendours on the outskirts of Paris, objected more specifically. 'The violence everywhere done to nature repels and wearies us', he complained. 'The saddest and most ungrateful of all places'. Yet among all the great gardens ever created in the world, Versailles has at least a fair claim to be the greatest, given its scale, its originality, its influence and – perhaps above all else – its absolutely empyrean cost. Besides, many find it beautiful.

Ian Thompson clearly falls into the latter category, but in a discriminating way. His comprehensive and sumptuous study* is far too sophisticated merely to retail praise. What he sets out to do – and succeeds brilliantly in doing – is to tell the complicated story of the making of Versailles as much in terms of the people involved in it – especially Louis XIV and his great *dessinateur* André Le Nôtre – as the developing, constantly changing gardens themselves. The physical details are not ignored, of course; it would be hard to better Thompson's descriptions of the way various elements, from the grand expanses of water to the most

---

* *The Sun King's Garden: Louis XIV, André Le Nôtre and the Creation of the Gardens of Versailles* By Ian Thompson (Bloomsbury)

intimate enclosed 'rooms', were conceived, designed, landscaped, and planted or built. But to be honest it isn't easy to keep them straight without a close acquaintance with the topography. What comes across more memorably is the human drama behind it all.

The Sun King was hardly the easiest client for any garden designer, but then André Le Nôtre was no commonplace gardener. Born in 1613 into a modestly-placed dynasty of professional plantsmen, Le Nôtre rose thanks both to his talents and his extraordinarily attractive personality. In a court where backbiting and subterfuge was a way of life, he seems to have attracted few enemies, eventually becoming as close as anyone to the great king himself. Part of the reason for his success, clearly enough, was Louis's own obsession with garden-making – garden-making, that is, on a truly regal scale.

Beginning in 1660, when Versailles consisted of little but a small château with a couple of parterres located among swamps and insignificant villages, the development of the site – at its apogee nearly 20,000 acres in extent – would take more than 30 years. Given Le Nôtre's placid, realistic disposition, satisfying the king's often frenetic demands must have been trying. Moreover, rather than merely a pleasure ground, Versailles gradually became an extension of Louis's sense of grandeur, a sort of vast psycho-political statement. Each new mistress, each fresh victory on the battlefield called for still more splendid structures, fountains, avenues, new proof in water, trees and marble that he was indeed *nonpareil* on the face of the earth. But his landscape designer was plainly up to the challenge.

From the start, Le Nôtre aimed for precision. Long vistas laid out with decisiveness, hedges cut with the accuracy of masonry, water features carefully designed to serve as mirrors – all these reflected the authority of his style. As Thompson remarks, 'tidiness and control were the essence of Le Nôtre's gardens, the perfect setting and metaphor for this orderly court'. Yet there were happy contrasts, too, the sylvan enclosures called *bosquet* where royal intimacies could be pursued or Watteauesque parties held, the beds of flowers that might be replanted twice a day for maximum effect.

It was of course wildly expensive. At one point in 1684, Thompson reports, as many as 36 *thousand* people were employed moving earth, laying pipe, and transplanting trees, many of them full-grown. Simply to furnish water for his fountains (they numbered 2,456 in the end), Louis commissioned major waterworks; one brought water to an altitude of 150 metres above the Seine at a cost of 3,500,000 *livres* (a single *livre* could buy you six litres of good wine), another – never completed – would have carried water overland 83 kilometres from the River Eure. That particular enterprise cost about nine million *livres* and the lives of thousands of workmen and soldiers. By the time Louis died in 1715, Versailles – and other royal gardens like that at Marly – had swallowed up a considerable portion of France's national wealth.

Strictly speaking, André Le Nôtre was not a gardener. He seems to have had no special fondness for unusual plants, producing his effects instead with a fairly narrow range of trees and hedging. His name has nevertheless gone down in history as a horticultural master, which I for one would not begrudge. Whether you like Versailles or not (which is a bit like asking whether the Grand

Canyon appeals to you), it deserves respect as representing one extreme of the world of gardening.

Somewhat closer to home is the work of two other royal gardeners, the two John Tradescants, father and son, who remain regrettably less well known than Le Nôtre. It is easy to see why from Jennifer Potter's doggedly researched book.* Where Le Nôtre's career, conducted in the full glare of the French court, is amply documented, the Tradescants' biography must be squeezed piecemeal out of obscure sources and tangential references. As a result *Strange Blooms* does not make for easy narrative reading, despite Potter's impressive labours. But the picture it paints of the seventeenth century gardening world is fascinating nonetheless.

The elder John Tradescant was born about 1570 – the exact date, like so much else, is uncertain. Nor is much known about how he gained the skills to become a gardener to the powerful Cecil family, overseeing development of their fine new estate at Hatfield House. Yet greatly skilled he obviously was, and trusted enough to be sent on plant buying expeditions to the Continent. From Hatfield he moved on to other important positions, among them gardener to the Duke of Buckingham, eventually becoming 'keeper of the royal gardens, vines, and silkworms' at King Charles I's palace of Oatlands. But as his talents for plantsmanship became better known, Tradescant's irrepressible curiosity about practically everything began to take over his life. He turned into a collector, and not just of plants.

As Potter shows vividly, by quoting not only from the fragmentary (and orthographically exotic) accounts by Tradescant but also by other (more literate) contemporaries, it was a yeasty time in the

* *Strange Blooms: The Curious Lives and Adventures of the John Tradescants* By Jennifer Potter (Atlantic Books)

realm of horticulture and exploration. The first few settlements in North America were being planted; travellers were venturing into Africa and the Far East. Tradescant himself managed a trip to Archangel, where he took careful note of the plants; on another occasion he joined an expedition to the Mediterranean against Barbary pirates. And though he never got to America, he made sure that explorer and merchant friends kept their eyes open there and elsewhere for anything that was, as he put it, 'strang', botanical and otherwise. Gradually, his house and garden in South Lambeth filled with rarities, from the Virginian spiderwort that was to bear his name to the hand of a mermaid to a cherrystone with eighty faces carved on it. No visit to London was complete without a tour of 'Tradescant's Ark'.

Meanwhile, John Tradescant the Younger was growing to manhood, following his father's footsteps. In 1637 he made the long and difficult journey to Virginia, apparently in part as an adventure and part as a serious plant-collecting expedition. (Potter effectively quashes the claim by earlier historians that he paid two other visits to Virginia.) Returning, he too became a gardener for Charles I, but had the misfortune to be so employed in 1649; though he didn't, like Charles, lose his head, he lost his job. By that time, however, he had added still more to the family museum, and could boast of having introduced many new species of plants to the gardens of England.

The sorry fate of the Ark rounds off the story. With both Tradescants dead, after a series of lawsuits a sharp-eyed and equally assiduous collector named Elias Ashmole succeeded in getting his hands on the whole lot. The affair was so distressing to John the Younger's widow that she drowned herself in the garden

Three Gardens

Hidcote is one of those very few iconic gardens, like Sissinghurst, that every self-respecting hortophile in England must visit. To Americans especially, it represents a kind of pinnacle of English garden-making, their interest and admiration accounting for a large proportion of the 150,000 gawkers who now tramp through the grounds each year. That it was created by an American in the first place, albeit a strange, secretive and thoroughly internationalized American, merely adds a note of mystery to the mix.

In the phrase of Fred Whitsey, the veteran garden writer whose handsome book* on Hidcote contains a short biography of Lawrence Johnston, the man himself 'remains an enigma'. Few papers, letters or other documents survived him; he never married; though he had friends in the gardening community he appears to have had few close acquaintances. After a Henry Jamesian upbringing in Europe as the child of rich expatriate Americans (rope, binding twine, banking), he chose to take British citizenship in 1892, and in 1907 bought a couple of hundred acres and a house on the northernmost end of the Cotswold scarp overlooking the Vale of Evesham. From then on, apart from service in the Northumberland Fusiliers in World War I (wounded, according to Whitsey, gassed and once left for dead), he devoted himself to Hidcote. He seems to have been a rather sad and lonely figure,

* *The Garden at Hidcote* By Fred Whitsey (Frances Lincoln)

mother-beset (she lived with him for decades, controlling the purse-strings and perversely leaving her fortune not to her son but to a trust). But for all that he was clearly a skilled plantsman and a garden designer of real genius.

While there has been some debate in recent years about the exact nature of Johnston's original creation at Hidcote – the National Trust took it over in 1948 and a number of changes were apparently made in restoring it – he evidently based his plans on the Arts and Crafts principles current among garden designers in Edwardian times. This called for a good deal of formal hedging to divide garden 'rooms', geometrical beds and pools, walls, and carefully controlled planting. At the same time, it involved a strongly romantic feeling, which today at Hidcote, with its richly mature trees and shrubs, can be almost overwhelming.

Where Johnston went beyond the conventions, however, was in his fascination with rare and unusual species. Not all of these survive today, of course, but the garden is still blessed with exceptional specimens, including a collection of old roses whose names sound like a roll call of society grandees of a century and a half ago. So taken was Johnston with collecting rare plants that he not only bankrolled plant-hunting expedition but actually went on a couple of them himself. One, with the great George Forrest to Yunnan, was a disaster; the two men fell out and Forrest, in fury, later wrote that he could not have found a worse travelling companion. 'Johnston is not a man, not even a bachelor, but a right good old spinster spoilt by being born male'. Still, even Forrest never claimed that Johnston couldn't build a garden, and Hidcote survives, beautifully, to prove it

* * * * * * *

The Morville Hours* is billed as garden writing, but it is garden writing only in the sense that Moby Dick is a treatise on whales. There is no need to have the slightest knowledge of or interest in horticulture to be enchanted by it. The author calls it 'this blackbird's nest of cobwebs and sheep's wool', which while unflattering and imprecise, does in its own idiosyncratic way convey a bit of its flavour.

It was in 1988 that Katherine Swift and her husband (an Oxford bookseller whose presence is curiously evanescent here) took a 20-year lease on the Dower House attached to a Shropshire estate called Morville Hall, a National Trust property. She quickly became obsessed with the place – its history, its setting at the head of Corve Dale, not far from Wenlock Edge and the Clee Hills, the village and countryside life going on around it. And as a veteran garden writer (as well as a rare book librarian and historical researcher) she decided to create a serious garden on an acre or so of adjoining rough grassland.

The making of this garden is the ostensible subject of her book. With a good bit of hard labour – and some local help – she plants hedges, lays out parterres and a maze, introduces new trees, flowers and rose beds, even constructs a long, narrow stone lined canal and a fountain. Predictably, it all takes years, and anyone who has ever tried to build a garden from scratch will be lost in admiration for her enterprise. At the same time, however, she is not particularly interested in explaining just how she did it. That *The Morville Hours* has something quite different in mind from

* *The Morville Hours* By Katherine Swift. (Bloomsbury)

the practicalities of, say, Margery Fish or Christopher Lloyd is clear from the way its nominal structure, like that of the garden itself, is overlaid with other shaping ideas. One is the notion of the yearly cycle, the great natural circle from winter to winter. Another is the sequence of monastic prayers in a medieval book of hours, also a circle. And a third, perhaps the most important but also the least obvious, is the author's own progression, season by season and year by year, to an understanding of her place in her family and in the history of Morville – and its transience.

All of which may sound pretty serious, if not pretentious, but Swift's touch is delicate and her writing nothing short of brilliant. She seldom misses an opportunity for a fascinating digression (you'll find wonderful short excursions on geology and local stone, beekeeping, the problem of 'sleepy' pears, early British Christians, pig culture and dragonflies, among others) and she is capable of some exquisite turns of phrase: Guernsey cows with 'the blades of their hips protruding through their tawny-gold hides like supermodels in blond cashmere'; a Robert le Diable rose is 'dark red…of a peculiarly livid and unstable colouring, streaked with crimson and grey and purple like macerated flesh'. The details have a Thoreau-like specificity – how it feels to be out on an icy winter's night smashing the ice in the canal so as to save the stonework from cracking, or the pleasures of mowing. More than the title connects *The Morville Hours* to the old prayerbooks with their brightly-coloured genre paintings of daily life. It displays the same richness, in words.

And the garden? It seems to have been conceived of as a kind of tribute to her horticultural predecessors, but exactly how is (appropriately) a bit vague. There is box hedging of the sort Romans might have planted, while other higher hedges are cut into arches to form a Norman cloister; Elizabethan knots front the house; a rose border celebrates Victorians; and there is a wild garden in the spirit of William Robinson, choked with camassia and *Campanula lactifolia* and rambling roses. Terrifying to keep up, which she admits. But gardens have come and gone at Morville in the past, and 'perhaps when the time comes I will hand it back to the field, a bit at a time, welcoming the wildness in...No garden is forever'.

* * * * * * *

Some forty miles southeast of Rome, at the foot of the steep western face of the Lepini Mountains, 'the most beautiful and romantic garden in the world' extends itself peacefully over sixteen lush, well-wooded acres. Seen from above, say from the village of Norma perched on the mountaintop, Ninfa appears essentially Italian, with an old square crenellated stone tower, a kidney-shaped lake, and dozens of cypresses rising up from the greenery like so many black exclamation marks. At ground level, the impression is radically different. Here, despite the cypresses and the ancient stonework, the garden is somehow more English than Italian – full of running water, roses, flowering trees, shade, and birdsong. Yet even this impression may mislead. Ninfa is in fact a garden like no other.

As Charles Quest-Ritson* makes clear, some of its character can be explained by its thoroughly international origins. It was created over several generations by the Caetani family, an

---

* *Ninfa: the Most Romantic Garden in the World* By Charles Quest-Ritson (Frances Lincoln)

aristocratic line of almost antediluvian age (and now, it seems, extinct) which for hundreds of years owned most of the territory for miles around. Falling on difficult times, they saw their fortunes restored, beginning in the nineteenth century by means of astute marriages, including several to Englishwomen. The 14th duke, Michelangelo Caetani married two (successively) and his son Onorato did even better, espousing the Hon. Ada Bootle-Wilbraham, the extremely well-connected niece of a British prime minister, herself a mountain-climber, balloonist, horsewoman – and gardener. The trend continued when in 1911 one of Ada's sons married a rich American, Margaret Gilbert Chapin.

This influx of foreign blood into the Caetani family had a notable effect: it stimulated what was already a modest inclination to create something horticulturally remarkable, and to do so on distinctly non-Italian lines. The focus of their efforts would be Ninfa which, long before it was a garden, was a village with one extraordinary feature – a huge spring yielding more than a thousand litres a second of clear fresh water, enough to fill a river big enough to harbour trout. It was, however, a ghost village, having been derelict since the fourteenth century. Wars, malaria (the Pontine Marshes, which lay between Ninfa and the sea, were still malarial until recent times), or bandits – no one knows exactly why, but according to Quest-Ritson, 'after 1381 Ninfa was never a town again'.

Instead, it was a splendid place for a garden. In the 1560s Cardinal Niccolo Caetani took advantage of the water and the abundance of tumbled stone to build a walled garden, subsequently abandoned; travellers in the nineteenth century (including Edward

Lear) found the place beautiful and wild and full of flowers. But although the Caetanis occasionally visited and picnicked there, it was Ada and her son Gelasio who first undertook serious garden-building after returning from World War I. Gelasio stabilized old ruined walls, and rebuilt the Gothic palace to live in; his mother began the ornamental plantings, particularly the roses that were her passion. By the mid-1930s, following the death of both Gelasio and Ada, the development of the garden fell into the hands of Roffredo, another of Ada's sons, his American wife Margaret (most of whose personal fortune went to supporting such cultural landmarks as the literary magazine *Botteghe Oscura*), and, eventually, their daughter Leila. It was at this point that Ninfa began to take on its present shape as a richly planted woodland garden, English but in a curious way delightfully expatriated.

And what is it like today? Well, it fully deserves the sort of superlatives that have been applied to it. It is difficult to imagine a more affecting place. Quest-Ritson speaks of its 'intimacy and mystery'; this may sound like waffle but strikes me as real enough. Perhaps it is the roses clambering over the old walls, their exuberance contrasting with the careful plantings of rare species of perennials, the huge aged trees balanced by the compact flowering cherries or the Japanese maples going scarlet in autumn, or the sparkling river and the many channels coursing through the lawns – it's hard to say just why it all works. But it certainly does.

Ninfa is now supported by a foundation and is open to the public to a limited extent. Whether it can survive or not, considering the threats from fire, area development or management less competent than that of the present director, a charming and brilliant man

HEROES AND OTHERS

The Tragedy of Vavilov

As a rule botany and politics don't interfere with each other. There are of course occasions when they connect tangentially – for example when the naturalist and plant hunter André Michaux carelessly got caught up serving as a volunteer spy in a hare-brained French scheme for chasing the Spanish out of the Mississippi Valley in the 1790s. (The scheme collapsed, leaving Michaux – and his plant collection – stranded.) Then there were the many diplomats and officials who made use of their political connections to clear their way for botanical exploration and collecting, from Augier Busbecq snaffling tulips in Ottoman Turkey to Sir George Staunton discreetly picking up the odd Chinese plant while travelling to Peking as part of the abortive Macartney Mission in 1792-94. But for the most part plants and politics don't mix, and if the tragic case of Nikolai Vavilov is in any way typical, it is clear that they shouldn't.

Not that Vavilov got involved on purpose. In fact, all the evidence indicates that he always did his level best to maintain a safe distance from politics. His misfortune was to be living in the Soviet Union at a time when Josef Stalin was running the place.

It would be hard to find a man who devoted himself and his entire career to the cause of plants and science more assiduously – and successfully – than Nikolai Ivanovich Vavilov. Trained as an agronomist, he graduated in 1911 with a particular interest in plant breeding, and was soon concentrating his considerable intellectual powers on the exciting new science of genetics. The subject was a controversial one. Although the German monk Gregor Mendel had worked out the basics of inheritance controlled by genes fifty years before, his work had been ignored at the time and only recently rediscovered. In its simplest form, Mendelism argued that certain characteristics reappear in successive generations in a predictable pattern controlled by forces (later termed genes) passed on by parents to their offspring. The genes, at least theoretically, remain unchanged from generation to generation, thus making it possible for plant breeders to in effect 'build' desirable characteristics into cultivars. Vavilov was fascinated by the possibilities this approach offered, especially after a year's study at Cambridge under the geneticist William Bateson.

It was at this point, back in Russia on the outbreak of World War I, that Vavilov began what would become a virtual obsession: collecting the widest possible variety of plant specimens in order to create a gene bank that could be used for breeding. It was a huge undertaking, involving what would be decades of travelling and searching out unknown strains. His country, battered by war and revolution, was desperately in need of food. Crop yields had to be improved and he was convinced that sophisticated breeding techniques based on genetics held the key. Disease resistance, survival in extremes of temperature and drought, vigour of growth – all these might be introduced from breeding stock to be found in remote places. It was clearly one way, perhaps the most direct way, to solve the looming problem of wholesale hunger.

During the next twenty years Vavilov collected plants and

seeds in some of the most inhospitable parts of the world. He trekked through the Pamirs in Central Asia, discovering unknown varieties of wheat, barley and rye in tiny isolated valleys; he ransacked the Crimea for fruit trees; he rounded up still more seeds in Afghanistan ('We cleaned out all of Afghanistan', he boasted), Abyssinia, North Africa and South America. His adventures were the stuff of legend. In a book recounting his travels he describes a near crash-landing in the middle of a Moroccan desert ('we were finally delivered to Oran in a half-conscious state') and the dangerous traverse of a glacier in Bukhara, leading frightened horses at a snail's pace over fissure-laced ice. In Taiwan, he found 'citrus fruits of gigantic proportions', in Kazakhstan he explored forests of wild apple trees. And everywhere, he collected.

Between journeys Vavilov set up dozens of experimental agricultural stations all over the Soviet Union, staffing them with young botanists eager to learn which species were most suited to differing soil and climate conditions. He also corresponded with botanists in foreign countries (pressing them for the latest scientific news and for more specimens), supervised slow and difficult hybridization, and ran the Institute of Plant Breeding, the country's principal botanical research establishment. In some ways an Indiana Jones type (though always dressed smartly in jacket and tie, even atop the Demi-Dhaurg glacier), he was nevertheless a serious scholar, competent in foreign languages, prolific in publications, and careful to stay up-to-date on the latest technical findings. His principal theoretical ideas derived from field work, such as the concept of geographical centres of diversity (wheat in Central Asia, maize in Mexico, potatoes in Peru and so forth) have proven to be lastingly valuable. Next to Ivan Pavlov (of Pavlov's dog), Vavilov was probably the Soviet scientist best-known and respected outside Russia in the years between the wars.

But his fame was to do him little good. In the 1930s, at the height of his achievements, he collided with politics – or rather with the combination of arbitrary power, fraudulence and sheer viciousness that passed for politics under the regime of Stalin. Curiously, there was a large element of scientific controversy involved too.

While Vavilov was busy travelling around the world and doing his best to build the world's finest collection of cultivated plants (the Institute in Leningrad eventually held 360,000 specimens, of which Vavilov himself collected 60,000), another agronomist of a distinctly different nature had been elbowing his way to prominence. Trofim Denisovich Lysenko came from peasant stock and though a reasonably competent farmer was only modestly educated, especially in comparison to Vavilov and the ranks of trained Soviet biologists. What he did have, in abundance, was ambition. An unsmiling man with a rat-like face and all the charm of a rattlesnake, Lysenko had the good fortune to be written up by *Pravda* in 1927 as an example of that wonderful new phenomenon – the 'barefoot scientist' untrammelled by formal knowledge who through his native skills could (it was said) solve the problems of agriculture much more readily than laboratory-bound specialists.

Lysenko's first claim to scientific fame was a theory that exposing seeds to cold and moisture (so-called 'vernalization') increased yields. While the technique worked only slightly or not at all, Lysenko gained a great deal of attention with it and other dubious ideas. He also became convinced that modern genetic thinking was all wrong, choosing instead to argue in favour of a radically different (and generally disdained) concept known as Lamarckism. The Lamarckists had no truck with genes. They believed that characteristics acquired by an organism during its life could actually shape its offspring's characteristics. As one anti-Lamarckian put it, it was as if someone losing an arm might expect to have one-armed children.

Whether or not it was the suggestion that changed social conditions might actually serve to change human nature in an essential way – a notion presumably appealing to Leninist philosophy – Lysenko and his Lamarckism caught Stalin's eye. The idea of a proletarian scientist appealed to the great leader, and Lysenko played the role with enthusiasm. As starvation spread across the Russian countryside in the wake of forced collectivization, he came up with one grand scheme after another for transforming agricultural output (none of which paid off), meanwhile boasting of the superiority of peasant knowledge over book learning. He made an actual fetish out of ignorance, refusing flatly to learn anything about genetics or to read scientific literature: 'It is better to know less, but to know just what is necessary for practical work'. Instead of the complex and lengthy process of genetic crossbreeding, Lysenko offered quick fixes. That they all failed, often disastrously, made no difference to his reputation. Stalin not only supported him publicly but, to the horror of the real scientists, gradually gave him more and more power over the scientific establishment. Vavilov saw his research stations closed or taken over by followers of Lysenko, and trained botanists, many of them world-famous, forced into retirement or worse.

It might be said that Vavilov was excessively innocent or short-sighted. He could never quite believe what was happening. He had avoided openly attacking Lysenko and had in fact tried to help him earlier in his career, but the younger man–perhaps for class reasons, perhaps out of jealousy or simple nastiness – had always pointedly opposed him. Now the difference was no longer purely scientific but personal. And as Lysenko's power grew the savagery of his opposition to Vavilov grew with it.

By the late 1930s Vavilov was despairing. He still hoped that reason and good science might win out but with Stalin's bloody show trials and the gradual destruction of the research structure he had built up that hope seemed frail. He was no longer allowed to leave the country on collecting expeditions. Lysenko, with powerful Kremlin backing, had cornered both the strongest bureaucratic positions in Soviet agriculture and most of the money available for research. Even in Vavilov's own institutes, Lysenko's minions noisily attacked gene theory. It was increasingly clear that the 'barefoot scientist' would settle for nothing less than Vavilov's absolute personal defeat. Unfortunately Lysenko had the means to achieve this.

For years the secret police had been assembling a dossier on Vavilov and planting spies among his colleagues. In 1940, with the encouragement of Stalin, the time to strike was ripe. In order to mask the seizure (Vavilov still had many friends in the scientific community abroad) he was allowed to make a collecting trip to the Ukraine; en route he was picked up by NKVD agents and silently dumped into the Lubyanka Prison in Moscow. He simply disappeared.

What happened next will be familiar to readers of thrillers.

As Mark Popofsky reports in his book *The Vavilov Affair*, an NKVD lieutenant named Khvat subjected Vavilov to months of intensive interrogation, with the express intention of breaking him. Thanks to fake documents and perjured evidence, Khvat succeeded; Vavilov was found guilty of leading an imaginary anti-Soviet organisation, of carrying on 'widespread wrecking activity aimed at disrupting and destroying the collective farm system and the collapse and decline of socialist agriculture in the USSR'. And spying for foreign countries. He was sentenced to be shot.

In the end, Nikolai Vavilov was not shot. After painful months on death row, in spite of pleading letters to the authorities by a few of his braver colleagues – and his own poignantly optimistic attempts to convince the Kremlin that he would undertake any work at all for the good of the Fatherland – he died in agony, feverish, after being moved briefly from his cell to a prison hospital. The cause was almost certainly starvation. He was 55. For a man who had devoted his life, literally, to a search for ways to prevent hunger, the irony is almost unbearable.

The Queer German

As a breed, plant hunters are a pretty strange lot. They need to be obsessives, for one thing, and it helps to be both psychologically and physically thick-skinned. While many of them are amiable souls, prepared to deal with their fellow men in the same spirit as they deal with plants, it has to be said that there are exceptions. One of the more exceptional, who stands out for his oddity as well as the fame he fortuitously achieved, has to be Friedrich Wilhelm Ludwig Leichhardt.

I first came upon Leichhardt under another name, in a book that has stuck firmly in my mind for years. Voss was what the Australian writer Patrick White chose to call him in his powerful, hallucinatory novel *Voss* (1957). Like the real Leichhardt, Voss is a botanist and an explorer venturing into the Antipodean wilderness in the 1840s. Also like the real Leichhardt, Voss is an improbable hero, glaringly ill-equipped to meet the challenges of the outback – the insects, the terrain, the savage climate and the equally savage and suspicious natives. But while the tale White tells does not accord exactly with Leichhardt's actual history – the book is built round a sort of long-distance imaginary love affair between Voss and a woman he scarcely met before setting out into the outback – it does offer a brilliant picture of the explorer's bizarre personality, and a chillingly plausible description of his still-mysterious fate.

Ludwig Leichhardt was born in 1813 in a small town in

Prussia. He seems to have been well-educated at several German universities. Although he was later to be known as 'Dr' Leichhardt, his medical competence proved to be minimal and there is no reason to think he got a degree. But he apparently did pick up a substantial understanding of botany and natural history. Wandering around Europe marked his young manhood; he lived by sponging off friends until in 1841 he decided to try Australia, having become a deserter by failing to show up for his mandatory German military service.

Australia in 1842, when Leichhardt arrived in Sydney, was a more or less unknown continent. A few small towns or settlements dotted the coastline, the era of penal colonies was just ending, and though some relatively accessible and salubrious country had been claimed for raising stock, much of the rest remained *terra incognita*. Its natural riches, from birds and plants and animals to mineral deposits, lay waiting to be discovered.

Leichhardt's attempts to capitalize on his scientific knowledge, however, came to nothing; his application for superintendent of the local botanical garden was turned down and he got no further when he tried to join a government exploration team. For a year or so he survived by giving lectures on botany and geology and accepting the hospitality of acquaintances, finally concluding that his future lay in exploring, alone if necessary. His first major trip, some 600 miles from a little north of Sydney to what is now Brisbane via an inland wilderness route, was in fact made on his own, and miraculously successful given that he had no bush experience and a bad sense of direction. But his botany proved to be first-rate. Emboldened, he decided on a large-scale expedition, all the way from the Darling Downs, west of Brisbane, to the northernmost tip of Arnhem Land near present-day Darwin.

In August 1844, having mustered a small group of companions this time (mostly inexperienced except for two aborigines and a young ornithologist named James Gilbert, who was to die en route), a herd of bullocks and other cattle (for pack transport and food), and horses, he set out. From the start there were problems – progress was slower than expected, the country rougher and drier, the animals kept straying. Packs were ripped and food lost when the little band attempted to force its way through dense thickets of acacia scrub. There were disputes among the men. Game was scarce and supplies inadequate. At one point they were reduced to sharing out a large lizard and a bandicoot as a day's rations for eight people. Trying out unfamiliar wild food through scientific curiosity or ignorance or simple hunger – figs, various beans and roots, unfortunate substitutes for coffee – the party was frequently prostrated by indigestion.

But they gradually made their way north. Leichhardt had calculated on seven months maximum for the journey; in fact it took more than fourteen before they finally stumbled into the isolated settlement of Port Essington on the coast. The whole party was beset by boils and festering sores. Towards the end, with most of the horses dead and only one bullock left ('poor Redmond' whom no one could contemplate killing), the probability of extinction must have seemed very high indeed.

Little of this sense of extreme peril comes into the account of the journey Leichhardt subsequently published after returning to Sydney, to great public acclaim. In *Journal of an Overland Expedition in Australia from Moreton Bay to Port Essington*, the picture he paints of his own leadership is consistently praiseworthy – difficulties overcome, dogged persistence in moving ever forward in spite of almost continuous hazards, careful record-keeping. The science is there, with dozens of new plants described. Admittedly his botanical orientation is toward food; flowers play a relatively minor role in his cataloguing and collecting. 'A fine eatable fruit of a purple colour' clearly counts for more than the discovery of a purely decorative plant (although he does note that 'a leguminous shrub, about five or six feet high, with purple blossoms…would be an ornament to our gardens'). Throughout, except for a faint note of self-congratulation and a curious failure to give any credit to his companions, he comes across as the very model of a modern explorer-plant hunter, though one with problems – the disastrous sudden loss of three hoses meant that he had to ditch most of his pressed and dried specimens.

Certainly his fame soared. Most people had long since given up hope for the expedition before it miraculously reappeared in Sydney. Public contributions poured in – Leichhardt himself got nearly £1500 and the others much smaller amounts in congratulatory prizes. The German government cleared him of draft-dodging. When he announced his new project – a trek clear across the continent from east to west, then down the coast to Perth – he had no trouble getting volunteers to come forward.

Once again the expedition started from Darling Downs. But progress was even more difficult than before. It was the wrong time of the year, rivers were flooded, the explorers suffered from fevers and flies that blinded them, food rotted, animals strayed.

What was worse, according to later testimony by survivors, Leichhardt himself began acting eccentrically. He stole food, gave way to emotional outbursts and stopped washing himself. The whole journey was to have taken two-and-a-half years, but after travelling some five hundred miles in five months, the expedition came to a halt and spent weeks recovering. Then it turned round and made its way painfully back to its starting point. Very little had been accomplished, although Daniel Bunce, a botanist member of the group, compiled a collection of more than a thousand plants, many hitherto unknown. If Leichhardt kept a journal this time, he never published it, perhaps out of embarrassment.

Leichhardt's standing as a leader, while not completely shattered, was now shaken. But not his ambition. Early in 1848, accompanied by two German friends, two or three Englishmen with bush experience, and a couple of aboriginals, he headed west, again intending to traverse the continent. This time he failed definitively. The expedition vanished, swallowed up in the vast desert wilderness of central Australia. Search parties came back empty-handed and though for many years rumours about his fate persisted, no solid information about what happened ever emerged. There is one clue: in about 1900 a small brass plate bearing his name was found attached to a partially-burnt shotgun hanging in a baobab tree near Sturt Creek on the edge of Western Australia, nearly two-thirds of the way to the west coast.

What sort of a man was Leichhardt? The question persists. The romance of his disappearance, combined with the huge fame his earlier successful expedition had engendered, made him better-known than a number of far more important figures in nineteenth century Australian exploration and science. At least one statue was erected in his honour. Yet there were always doubts, stirred up in part by accounts by some of those who had accompanied him and came to dislike him. Possibly the most savage blow to his reputation came nearly a hundred years after he had disappeared, when a writer named Alec Chisholm, a distinguished Australian ornithologist, succeeded in tracking down the lost diary of John Gilbert, the man who died during the Port Essington trek. Gilbert was the veteran of several earlier bush sorties before joining Leichhardt and seems to have acted as Leichhardt's second-in-command. But halfway through the trip north he was killed by an aboriginal spear during a surprise nighttime attack.

Chisholm was fascinated and appalled by Leichhardt. In his eyes, Gilbert had been unfairly neglected and Leichhardt grotesquely over-ranked. The book Chisholm wrote, *Strange New World*, proposes to be a defence of Gilbert's exceptional accomplishments as a pioneer of Australian ornithology, but is in effect a broadside attack on Leichhardt – his claimed achievements, his competence as a leader, his grasp of science and of bush skills. Nothing he did was sensible. He is always 'wandering aimlessly'. He is a terrible shot and ludicrously insists on always wearing a sword. His plotting of locations is inaccurate, his botany dubious, his willingness to eat anything, from maggotty meat to bad fruit disgusting. Some of what the author reports comes from Gilbert's journal (though Gilbert is on the whole far less critical of Leichhardt, at least until well into the journey), more from other memoirs or enemies of the man Chisholm calls 'the queer German', most of whom had something to complain about. There is no attempt at all at a balanced account. The result is intensely readable if startling in its venom. Even Ludwig Leichhardt couldn't have been *that* bad.

It was Chisholm's *Strange New World* that gave Patrick White his lead in creating Voss, though he used his imagination when he described the expedition's tragic end at the hands of angry aborigines. But White's version of Leichhardt is not meant to be literal; as he says in a letter to his publisher, 'I only based my explorer on Leichhardt. The latter was, besides, merely unusually unpleasant, whereas Voss is mad as well'. And in the novel, mad he certainly is. No use looking to White for any kind of rehabilitation. The best that can be said is that the novelist viewed his character with some sympathy. At the end of the book, an old comrade muses: 'Voss? No. He was never God, though he liked to think he was. Sometimes, when he forgot, he was a man'.

In recent years there have been some signs that 'the queer German' might once again have his day. Further studies have established that at the time of his arrival in Australia, he really was a well-trained scientist, perhaps the best ever to have reached the continent. His plant collections en route to Port Essington were indeed substantial, amounting to four or five thousand specimens, and had he not been forced to discard a large proportion when his horses were killed, his discoveries might be much better known. As a leader he may have been eccentric, but the fact remains that except for poor Gilbert, who fell to an aboriginal spear, no one died under his command until the final, mysterious, comprehensive disaster. Few explorers in the bitter wastes of Australia could claim that.

A Floral Orgy

An old saying among American publishers used to have it that three subjects were certain to sell – Abraham Lincoln, doctors and dogs. All you needed to do to beat the charts was to publish a book about Lincoln's doctor's dog. There's no reason to think that the London publisher Joseph Johnson had the exact same gimmick in mind in April 1789 when he issued a volume devoted to two other popular subjects, flowers and sex, but he may as well have. Erasmus Darwin's poem *The Loves of the Plants* was a vast success, propelling the corpulent Derbyshire doctor into national fame. Had there been a bestseller list at the time, the book would probably have gone straight to the top of it. This in spite of its unlikely form – thousands of often graceless rhyming couplets, liberally embellished with footnotes running in some cases to many hundreds of words, on subjects ranging from Arkwright's spinning jenny to meteorology. 'I hear nothing but praise and congratulation', the novelist Maria Edgeworth wrote to Darwin.

But if Darwin's success was unlikely, it was not altogether unpredictable. The connection between sex and flowers was very much in the air in the late eighteenth century, thanks to the Swedish botanist variously known as Carol Linné, Carol von Linné, Linneus, or – most commonly – Linnaeus. For Linnaeus had come up with a system of classifying plants according to their sexual characteristics, and the idea – and all the ramifying notions that went with it –

clearly fascinated Darwin, along with most of Europe's intellectual community.

In any case, there is no doubt that Erasmus Darwin had a taste for sex. He fathered at least twelve children, including two illegitimate daughters, and for the time his attitudes were extremely liberal. He had no problem with homosexuality or even masturbation, and as a medical man regarded intercourse as an excellent remedy for hypochondria. And though he was overweight, with smallpox scars and a severe stammer, he seems to have been, improbably, very attractive to women. At the age of nearly fifty, against considerable local competition, he succeeded in gaining the hand of a beautiful and much younger widow as his second wife.

Apart from sex, however, Darwin was also profoundly interested in plants. He had his own botanic garden a mile from Lichfield, a town where he had spent most of his life and became famous as a physician. (He was such a well-known doctor, in fact, that George III wanted him to be his personal physician, but Darwin would not leave the Midlands for London.) His interests spanned a vast array of topics. As a key member of the Lunar Society, the group of Birmingham 'philosophers' so well described recently by Jenny Uglow in her book *The Lunar Men*, he was curious about virtually anything scientific. Coleridge, no friend to Darwin's poetry ('I absolutely nauseate Darwin's poem', he declared firmly) nevertheless allowed that the doctor possessed 'a greater range of knowledge than any other man in Europe'.

Botany, however, remained a particular love. In the early 1770s, not long after the death of his first wife, Darwin formed the Lichfield Botanical Society, with the aim of translating the works of Linnaeus. This society (an exiguous one, consisting of Darwin himself and just two others) would in years to come turn a number of texts by Linnaeus from Latin into English, among them the key text *Species Plantarum.* It was here that Darwin found the raw material for his *Loves of the Plants* and, as he put it, was driven to 'inlist Imagination under the banner of Science'.

Given his fascination with plants and science in general, Darwin's involvement with Linnaeus's work was inevitable. No one presuming to an interest in botany could be ignorant of his theories and writings. Over a period of some 45 years the Swede had published a series of books that progressively developed an organised picture of nature – plants, animal, even minerals – and in the course of doing this devised a method of naming altogether simpler and more practical than any used before. This so-called binomial system would be his most lasting achievement. Where for example a catmint might once have had to answer to the mind-twisting name of *Nepeta floribus interrupte spicatus pedunculatis* ('Nepeta with flowers in an interrupted pedunculated spike') thanks to Linnaeus could now be spoken of as plain *Nepeta cataria,* with a considerable saving in breath and space on garden markers. It was a clear stroke of genius.

But what moved Erasmus Darwin most was Linnaeus's attempt to organise the overgrown jungle of the plant world by means of a new classification system. It was a peculiarly attractive one. Since Aristotle and the Greeks, natural scientists had been trying to achieve such a system, never with much success, and now that new plants were being discovered in all parts of the globe in truly overwhelming numbers, the difficulty of distinguishing them unambiguously had become acute. Linnaeus's solution was straightforward. Study and experimentation had convinced him that plant reproduction was sexual, and that male and female organs were represented in nearly all plants by stamens (male) and pistils (female). Plants differed by the number of these elements. Simply by counting them, he concluded, and further considering such features as whether the stamens are conjoined, whether pistils and stamens are found in the same flower, or whether the stamens are all of the same height, it was possible to build up a comprehensive taxonomic system consisting of twenty-four distinct classes.

As a practical solution to a large problem, and one which in its simplicity made it especially appealing to amateurs who enjoyed the idea of playing botanist, the Linnean system quickly became popular. It did not, however, receive a universal welcome. For one thing, some botanists still regarded plant sexuality as nonsense, and wholly unproved. Others objected that the system did nothing to explain the relationships between species and was completely artificial – even classing all trees or all blue flowers together made more sense. And then there was the problem of decency. Sex is unsettling at the best of times, and Linnaeus had not made things easy. Darwin would compound the issue with *Loves of the Plants*.

Although Linnaeus wrote in Latin, he was outspoken, and like many contemporary biologists had an unfortunate liking for analogy. He had no hesitation in describing the male and female organs as 'husbands and wives' and the calyx as 'the marriage bed'. The twenty-four classes he proposed were full of such off-colour descriptions as multiple husbands and hermaphrodites, shared (or separate) beds, concubines and clandestine marriages. Translators, among them Erasmus Darwin, carried the process of personification even further with a rough Georgian enthusiasm. (One of Darwin's advisors, if briefly, was Samuel Johnson, a neighbour in Lichfield. Perhaps that helps explain some of the vigour.) The result, while vividly intelligible, was shocking to those of a delicate disposition. Talking about plants as vegetation was one thing, but describing their sexual activities in human terms quite another. Victorian prudery, while not yet fully developed, was on the way.

While Linnaeus's treatment was, for some, unsettling, at least his metaphors made his subject clear. Darwin's intention in writing *Loves of the Plants* was apparently to make it clearer yet. Convinced that Linnaeus had really hit upon a definitive explanation of the way the plant world should be viewed through sex, Darwin would employ this incendiary subject matter in the service of art. And, along the way, give fresh publicity to the Linnean system.

It was apparently Anna Seward, a Lichfield poet friend and fellow gardener, who gave him the idea of writing about the plants in his botanic garden. He took it up enthusiastically. 'The Linnean system is unexplored poetic ground', he declared, 'and a happy subject for the muse'. With this in mind he launched his poem. It took him years; while working full time as a doctor and simultaneously translating Linnaeus, he gradually accumulated sections of his poem, scribbling on bits of paper as he jolted over the countryside on house calls in his special glass-roofed carriage.

Reading *The Loves of the Plants* today, it is sometimes hard to keep a straight face. Narrated in the voice of a 'Botanic Muse', it in some ways it resembles a kind of bizarre flora, in which Darwin ticks off one after another plant to illustrate the Linnaean categories, all the while making poetical play with their sexual characteristics as if they were groups of humans. Canna, for instance, is virtue itself, with one male (stamen) and one female (pistil) 'plighting their nuptial vow'. Broom, on the other hand, with ten stamens and a single pistil, suggests something less conventional:

> Sweet blooms GENISTA in the myrtle shade,
>
> And *ten* fond brothers woo the haughty maid.

In lychnis, Darwin observes the five pistils rising above the petals, 'as if looking abroad for their distant husbands' (the ten stamens), and things can get heated:

> Each wanton beauty, trick'd in all her grace
>
> Shakes the bright dew-drops from her blushing face;
>
> In gay undress displays her rival charms,
>
> And calls her wondering lovers to her arms.

With six males and one female, Gloriosa provides a scene involving toy-boys:

> Proud GLORIOSA led three chosen swains,
>
> The blushing captives of her virgin chains. –
>
> – When Time's rude hand a bark of wrinkles spread
>
> Round her weak limbs, and silver'd o'er her head,
>
> Three other youths her riper years engage,
>
> The flatter'd victims of her wily age.

Then there are plants like adonis (pheasant's eye) whose stamens and pistils are numerous enough to evoke a full-scale orgy, or at least a mass marriage on Moonie scale:

> A hundred virgins join a hundred swains,
> And fond ADONIS leads the sprightly trains;
> Pair after pair, along his sacred groves
> To Hymen's fane the bright procession moves...
> – Thick, as they pass, exulting Cupids fling
> Promiscuous arrows from the sounding string;
> On wings of gossamer soft Whispers fly,
> And the sly glance steals side-long from the eye.
> – As round his shrine the gaudy circles bow,
> And seal with muttering lips the faithless vow,
> Licentious Hymen joins their mingled hands
> And loosely twines the meretricious bands.

It must not be thought that Darwin confined himself to floral analogies in verse. His poetry was meant to do more than merely entertain. Whenever an opportunity presented itself for a prose footnote (the longer the better) he seized it, describing the actual plant concerned, its place in the Linnaean system, and practically anything else that seemed pertinent, including much that wasn't (but is usually engaging). This material, which is often more fun to read than the poem it annotates, showed him to be a keen and accurate botanist, as well as a man determined to explore difficult larger questions of biology and other sciences. Two years after publishing *The Loves of the Plants* he joined it with another long work called (rather misleadingly) *The Economy of Vegetation.* Couched in the same high-flown style, replete with sylphs and gnomes, it undertakes a broad poetic survey of the entire world of natural history. Splendid footnotes deal with everything from fire engines to cotton gins, and include the sad story of one Dr Richman of Petersburgh, who tried Franklin's kite in a thunderstorm; 'receiving the lightning in his head with a loud explosion, [he] was struck dead amid his family'.

For all Darwin's efforts, and those of other botanists who found the Linnaean system of classification of great use at the time, it gradually fell out of favour in the face of more sophisticated schemes. Today taxonomy is still in a state of flux as we learn more about the genetic relationships between species. What has survived is Linnaeus's brilliantly ingenious binomial naming gambit. As for Erasmus Darwin, his name has suffered a stranger fate. Practically the only Darwin the world knows today is his grandson Charles.

Two Remarkable Women

If insects inherit the earth – and given our present fecklessness it seems entirely possible that they will – one reason may be the extraordinary process known as metamorphosis. As Kim Todd points out in the introduction to her brisk biography of the German painter Maria Sibylla Merian,* who gained fame for her almost hallucinogenic paintings of natural subjects, insects are already the most successful of living creatures. A million species are known; another four or five million, it is estimated, are yet to be discovered. Their most powerful advantage over the rest of creation is their ability to take on radically different forms at different stages of life, thus reducing competition for food and space. A leaf-eating earth-bound caterpillar transforms itself into an aerial butterfly living on nectar, a maggot turns into a fly: this is metamorphosis.

In the seventeenth century, when Merian was born, metamorphosis was a mystery. Along with many natural phenomena, such as the migration of birds or the generation of insects, it had never come in for much serious scientific attention or, for that matter, serious attention of any kind. Quoting classical authorities still had the edge over experimentation, and in any case, who was prepared to believe that a living animal could change its form utterly between youth and maturity?

---

* *Chrysalis: Maria Sibylla Merian and the Secrets of Metamorphosis*
By Kim Todd (I. B. Tauris)

The world Maria Sibylla Merian entered in 1642 was still in many ways deeply medieval. The Thirty Years War was grinding to a close, leaving northern Europe ruined. Yet renaissance was in the air – the family's trade was printing and publishing. It specialized in illustrated books, making it natural for her to learn to paint, especially when her widowed mother married a painter. Guild rules in Frankfurt meant that women were not allowed to use oil paints, but watercolours were all right, and young Maria soon developed marked skill. Her subjects were the usual flowers and – what was more unusual – insects. Her roses had larvae, her hyacinths caterpillars. Moreover, they were exactly true to life.

But her fascination with insects did not stop with painting them. Somehow, having observed them closely in her own garden, she was no longer prepared to accept conventional wisdom about their origin and lives. (One accepted theory of how to 'get' a bee: 'Find a sunny space roofed with tile; beat a three year old bull to death; put poplar and willow branches under the body; cover it with thyme and serpellium; the bees will emerge'.) The enigma of metamorphosis particularly exercised her. Collecting caterpillars and maggots, she recorded in sketches and paintings the stages they passed through as they turned into moths, butterflies or flies.

Meanwhile, she had her own life to lead. As Todd points out, detailed biographical evidence is difficult to come by – Merian left very little written record – but some facts are clear. At sixteen she married a painter and had two daughters. The union was rocky from the start. Living in Nuremberg, she taught flower painting to well-born young ladies and published her own first *Blumenbuch*, but her real interest was less in the flowers than in the creatures in, around, and on them. In 1679 came the first fruit of this interest, a wholly new kind of illustrated volume entitled *The Caterpillar's Wondrous Metamorphosis*. It has flowers, of course. But it also has insects in various stages of change from caterpillar to 'summer-bird' (butterfly) – rendered with electrifying precision. This was art; it was also science.

In 1685, her husband having left the scene, Merian, her daughters and her mother chose to join the fringe Protestant sect known as the Labadists and move to its commune in a castle in West Friesland. No one knows quite why they did this, but the era was rife with more or less extreme religious groups. In any event, during the six years she spent there she continued with her insect studies in spite of the strict discipline; so far as she was concerned, the work was 'godly'. The commune, however, faltered and gradually fell apart. The family moved to Amsterdam.

Now, in middle age, Merian found herself at last in touch with modern intellectual currents. She earned her keep in Amsterdam by teaching, selling flower paintings and acquiring patrons; there was less time for experiments. Yet dead specimens, the sort that might be seen under glass or pinned in cases in the *wunderkammer* of connoisseurs, would simply not serve her purpose. She needed to paint from life, no matter how awkward it might prove. Moreover, she was determined to round off her years of research into metamorphosis. In 1699, at the age of fifty-two, she made the unprecedented decision to travel to the Surinam jungles where, she knew, a vast array of new plants and insects awaited observation.

What we know about the expedition is limited to the short commentaries appended to the paintings she published after her return in *Metamorphosis Insectorum Surinamensium*. The country was now in the hands of the Dutch (having been exchanged with the British for New York in 1667) and there were connections with the Labadists, who had tried to establish colonies there. For the lady naturalist-painter, however, nothing was easy. Snakes, heat, disagreeable insects, thorns, disease, the impossibility of climbing into the rainforest canopy where so much of interest went on – all these were challenges she had to meet. Preceded by slaves wielding machetes, clambering up ladders to reach webs full of caterpillars, she collected and sketched. She had expected to stay five years, but sickness – perhaps malaria or yellow fever – drove her back to Europe after two. Still, she took with her not only many crates of specimens (which would be sold) but hundreds of beautiful paintings destined for publication.

After Merian's death in 1717 (with yet another caterpillar book nearly finished) her reputation suffered from many poor and careless reprintings of her pictures. Colours faded, sequences were jumbled. The accuracy and beauty of the original paintings, held privately in collections scattered from St. Petersburg to Windsor, was forgotten. Only now, with the publication of facsimiles in recent years, and exhibitions of such sequestered masterpieces as those George III somehow acquired in the eighteenth century, has it been possible to appreciate the extraordinary accomplishments of this extraordinary woman.

* * * * * * *

Near the beginning of her biography of Henrietta Luxborough (1699-1756)*, Jane Brown remarks that she was a woman who

---

* *My Darling Heriott: Henrietta Luxborough, Poetic Gardener and Irrepressible Exile* by Jane Brown (Harper Press)

'lived in the lee of history'. Just so: her half-brother was the reprobate politician and philosopher Henry Bolingbroke; her husband's fortune stemmed from the greatest financial scandal of the age, the South Sea Bubble; her ancestral blood was as blue as any in England. Yet – and this is the tragedy not only of Henrietta's own life, but also of Brown's otherwise scholarly and well-meant biography – nothing much of real interest, historical or otherwise ever happened to her. Stirring events and important cultural connections simply passed her by. A born victim – of eighteenth century male chauvinism, of circumstance, and (at one critical juncture) of her own fecklessness – she had what must be regarded as a sad, unfulfilled life. Her one success was her garden.

Practically from birth she was fixated by her glorious half-brother, watching him rise meteorically to a title and power under Queen Anne. But as Bolingbroke rose, he fell, ending in exile in France after unwisely backing the Stuarts. This coincidentally had consequences for Henrietta. Among those Harry met in Paris was a rich young man named Robert Wright, son of one of the more culpable South Sea Bubble crooks then sheltering abroad from English law. Harry apparently suggested a match with his sister.

The marriage was never a happy one, though it produced two children. Wright (who later took the title Luxborough) became increasingly difficult, showing little affection for his wife and amusing himself elsewhere. For her part, Henrietta made do by paying visits to several women friends who, like her, enjoyed corresponding in verse. She scarcely saw her children.

In 1734, while staying with a friend, Lady Hertford, near

Windsor, she made an innocent mistake that would change her life. Also at the house was a handsome young tutor named John Dalton. Dalton fancied himself a poet too, and – though Henrietta was ten years his senior – they soon found themselves exchanging verses. There was almost certainly no affair. But the poetry so pleased Lady Hertford that she copied it into her commonplace book, where – inevitably – other house guests, and possibly Henrietta's husband, saw it.

However he learned about Dalton, Luxborough reacted violently. A humourless, rigid man with a highly developed sense of his own importance, he first sent Henrietta to a remote village, then had her locked up in their London house. But rumours of scandal spread nevertheless, elaborated in the telling. Henrietta was helpless. Finally Luxborough laid down his decision. She would be banished to Warwickshire, to a house he owned called Barrells. She would be forbidden access to her children and not allowed to travel to London. She lived the rest of her life there, alone.

It could not have been a happy existence, but she seems to have made the best of it. She had always been interested in gardening, and the grounds offered 'capabilities', as the great landscapist Lancelot Browne would have said. She made woodland walks and a shell grotto, built a fake hermitage, installed urns and other features; her ha-ha allowed the fields and distant hills to seem part of her garden; and her plantings, such as is known of them, may have anticipated Gertrude Jekyll a hundred years later. Compared to the magnificent spreads being created by men like Henry Hoare at Stourhead or Lord Cobham at Stowe, of course, hers was modest indeed, but it apparently attracted the admiration of those few of her contemporaries who knew about it.

One who did, and whose own gardening exploits brought him a considerably greater measure of fame, was the poet William Shenstone. Thirty miles to the west of Barrells, in what is now a suburb of Birmingham, he created the Leasowes, an elaborated rural landscape garden he called a *ferme ornée*. Henrietta was fascinated by him (he rather less by her) and their letters dealing with shrubbery or the niceties of ornamental sculpture and Latin inscriptions breathe the spirit of Georgian connoisseurship. To the extent that Henrietta Luxborough is known at all these days, it is probably largely due to her connection with Shenstone.

The author of seven other books on garden history, Jane Brown is naturally eager to establish her subject's importance as an innovator in the world of horticulture and design. We are left unconvinced. She never wrote anything (except letters and a quantity of bad poetry), apparently influenced no one, and there is no reason to think that her garden was in any way really adventurous. After her death it simply vanished, and its subsequent history, doggedly searched out by Brown, serves perfectly to show how time destroys not only gardens but also our chances of knowing about them with any degree of exactitude. Yet as a survivor of an often savage social system, Henrietta Luxborough is interesting, even admirable. That may be reason enough for this careful and devoted biography.

Anglo-Florentines

In 1855, the Goncourt brothers described Florence as *'ville toute Anglaise'* which, though slightly inaccurate because there were plenty of Americans on hand too, was close to the truth. For those Anglo-Saxons with money and time on their hands (and a taste for art, and the fashionable medieval) Florence was the place to come – and if possible, to settle. Beginning with the fall of Napoleon and increasing as the century wore on, thousands fled depressing northern climates and unromantic homelands for this old and deeply charming city. As Katie Campbell notes in her beautifully-written account,* by 1869 30,000 of Florence's 200,000 inhabitants were either British or American.

The most favoured of all, generally meaning those wealthy enough to be spared financial worries, were the expatriates who purchased villas on the hills surrounding the city and restored them, creating private elysiums complete with gardens, historical resonance and nightingales. *Villeggiatura*, the rural retreat, had a long tradition in Italy; Florence in summer was uncomfortably hot (it still is) and in pre-plumbing days must have been unspeakable for other reasons too. So when the Anglos began arriving, there were dozens of more or less derelict suburban villas just waiting for rescue. Many dated back to the fifteenth century or before. Like the ancient city itself, they appeared to be blessed with literary and

---

* *Paradise of Exiles: The Anglo-American Gardens of Florence* By Katie Campbell (Frances Lincoln)

the best-known today, and his Settignano villa I Tatti most celebrated. Arriving in Florence in 1888, a young art expert with a commission to buy paintings for his Boston patron Isabella Stewart Gardner, he soon built a comfortable fortune locating and certifying masterpieces on behalf of wealthy buyers (and himself). The villa, once a simple farmhouse, and its spectacular gardens were transformed with the help of a talented architect named Cecil Pinsent, who later became the guru-of-choice to the whole exile community. When Berenson died, full of honours, in 1959, he willed I Tatti to Harvard University for a study centre. (The same useful fate befell several of the 17 villas described here).

Campbell is particularly drawn to some of the stranger characters among the Anglo-Florentines. They include Sir George Sitwell (who in her memorable phrase had an attraction to 'foetid romanticism' and wrote a classic book, *On the Making of Gardens*, that praises 'neglect, desolation and solitude'); Mabel Dodge Luhan, about whom Gertrude Stein wrote an incomprehensible 'cubist word-picture in verse', who spent only eight years at her Villa Curonia before getting bored and proceeding to marriage with a Pueblo Indian in Taos, New Mexico; Sybil Cutting, one of the *Americani con soldi* (Americans with money), who entertained Pre-Raphaelite painters in the same rooms of her Villa Medici where Leonardo da Vinci and his fellows had met four hundred years before; and Sir Frederick Stibbert, who had a fondness for dressing up in the medieval armour he collected. Then there was the reclusive and mysterious Princess Ghika, described as hating 'both men and mankind', and as owner of Villa Gamberaia was responsible for what is now according to Campbell 'the most perfect small garden in Tuscany'. Florence was a magnet for popular writers, though little is known about most of them, including even the location of their villas and gardens; the most engaging of these must be Joseph Lucas, whose 1913 *Our Villa in Italy* turned out to be smash best-seller on the order of *A Year in Provence*. It chronicled his adventures restoring a villa in Florence and must have appealed to the same market as Peter Mayle – those who dream of ancient houses in the sun.

Luther Burbank

Icons fade. When I was a kid in the 1930s, Thomas Edison was still a name to drop; my father was proud of having met him, a fact he told me more than once. I don't believe my father ever met Luther Burbank, but you can be sure I'd know it if he had. Just as Edison represented the archetypical inventor, the man who had thought up everything from the electric light bulb to the phonograph, Luther Burbank was famous as the magician with plants, the man who came to mind first whenever anybody mentioned new species of vegetables or fruit. Edison remains known, in a rather antique way – you can visit his shed-like laboratory, moved bodily from New Jersey to Greenfield Village near Detroit by Henry Ford, another passé icon. But poor Luther, in this day of genetic engineering and protoplast fusion, can no longer claim much popular attention. It's a pity, and a more complicated story than might first appear.

I had pretty much forgotten about Burbank too, until last summer. We were driving rather aimlessly north of San Francisco, having visited the Napa Valley and an unhealthy number of vineyard tasting rooms, when we came into a prosperous little city called Santa Rosa. Santa Rosa, it turned out, was where Luther Burbank had lived for fifty years, and where he had conducted his plant breeding work. (He also had an experimental farm seven miles away in the Santa Rosa Valley.) His house and the garden surrounding it – now reduced from its original four acres to 1.6 – have been pleasantly preserved as a memorial.

It wouldn't do to make too much of this. Santa Rosa hasn't. The garden occupies a flat city block and has few sizeable trees. Though the central area was redesigned forty years ago to incorporate a fountain in the middle of a circular screened area, while borders of roses and perennials suggest decorative impulses, the general impression is still that of a plantsman's laboratory. Raised rectangular demonstration beds contain examples of plant varieties he worked with, there is a small orchard of hybrid fruit and nut trees, and a greenhouse almost as big as the house (which is, after all, not much more than a cottage). You get the distinct feeling that design, as such, didn't interest Burbank much; what he wanted was plenty of sun, adequate water, and room to grow things. Santa Rosa was beautifully equipped to supply these – 'I firmly believe', he was supposed to have declared on arrival there in 1876, 'from what I have seen that this is the chosen spot of all this earth as far as nature is concerned' – and grand gardeners could stay or leave.

Like most nineteenth century Californians, Burbank was born an Easterner – in rural Massachusetts in 1849, coincidentally at just about the time the Gold Rush was getting underway. His fascination with plants began early, stimulated by an uncle who was a geologist, and by the time he was seventeen he was already experimenting with grafting, seed selection and even, tentatively, crossbreeding. Evolutionary ideas made a powerful impact on his adolescent thinking, particularly Charles Darwin's 1868 *Animals and Plants under Domestication*. With the death of his father, however, there was no money for further education, and he was forced to depend for his living on his skills as a nurseryman. Leasing a few acres as a market garden, he set about raising vegetables and seed for sale.

It must have been a frustrating situation for a would-be scientist, but Burbank used what time he could spare for tinkering with bean and corn (maize) varieties. Then he had a stroke of luck. He noticed a seed ball, like a miniature tomato, ripening on an Early Rose potato plant. He had never known Early Rose to bear seed before, and the phenomenon is rare in any case; potatoes are, of course, normally propagated by sowing saved tubers – cloned, in effect. The prospect of having some potato seeds to play with excited him. He didn't think much of available varieties and seeds offered the possibility of cross breeding. Though at one point the seedball fell off and vanished, to be found again only after days of panicky searching, he ended up with twenty three plausible-looking potato seeds. Planted out the following spring, all germinated, with surprising results. The tubers on twenty one vines were worthless – distorted, lumpy, small – but two were attractive, and one of these truly exceptional, smooth, large and white. Moreover, when planted again the next season, the best one multiplied readily. Burbank found himself with a half bushel of the finest potatoes anyone had ever seen.

Unlike the hundreds of deliberately engineered hybrids he later produced, what came to be known as the Burbank Seedling was basically a fortunate discovery, and he never claimed anything else for it. It did, however, make his name. A year later he sold the rights to a Marblehead seed merchant (for $150, though he wanted

$500); the strain subsequently became, in a slightly improved version called the Burbank Russet, the most widely grown potato in America, which it still is. (All MacDonald's fries are made from it.) The money gave Burbank the courage to shake the dust of Massachusetts from his heels and set out for California.

He arrived in Santa Rosa in 1872, equipped with little but a parcel of books and clothing and ten of his special potatoes the dealer had allowed him to keep. Life there, despite the comfortable climate, was difficult. He had to work as a carpenter to make ends meet. But before long he had set up as a nurseryman and was also selling his potatoes. With a solid grounding in grafting and horticulture he gradually made a success of the enterprise, partly because he was prepared to take gambles. On one occasion he accepted a commission, turned down by other nurserymen, to produce 20,000 prune trees in only eight months. Bud-grafting onto quick-sprouting almond seedlings, he succeeded in meeting the deadline.

Burbank was determined to pursue his real vocation, plant breeding, and by 1890 he could afford to devote all his energies to it. He believed that the right way to go about it was sheer quantity – collect as many varieties as possible (in some cases from abroad, wherever he could recruit helpers to send him specimens) and make as many crosses as possible, selecting the most promising offspring and then, after dumping the rejects, repeating the process. His gardens eventually filled with thousands of plants, flowers, vegetables and trees in various stages of experimentation. When he came up with what he considered to be an improved variety, he would sell it to other nurserymen and seedsmen to be placed on the market. The partial list of his 'novelties' is staggering: no fewer than 113 plums and prunes, three dozen blackberries and raspberries, quinces, plumcots (a cross between plums and apricots, which experts had said couldn't be done), apples, peaches, chestnuts, nectarines, grapes, and even three new walnuts, to say nothing of tamed garden varieties of Shasta daisy (*Leucanthemum x superbum*).

One of Burbank's most ambitious and widely-reported undertakings was his search for a spineless cactus. Begun towards the end of the nineteenth century, it continued for years and was, as he put it, 'the most arduous and soul-testing experience that I have ever undergone'. The problem, naturally, was the prickles. The cactus flowering season, when the crosses had to be pollinated by hand, 'was a period of torment for me both day and night'. But he was convinced that a spineless cactus could be the ultimate forage crop, serving cattle and sheep in desert areas with both food and water. In the end he proudly succeeded in growing a giant smooth *Opuntia* and with some fanfare announced it to the world.

That Burbank's dream of feeding all the cows in Arizona on prickle-free cactus came to nothing is in a way a portent of what would happen to his reputation. Other research soon showed that while spinelessness could be achieved in a well-watered and fertile garden in Santa Rosa, under more stressed desert conditions cacti would be as rebarbative as ever, and too slow-growing to be useful in any case. What was left of the experiment was, as usual, the publicity.

Nobody would call Luther Burbank a modest man. He published catalogues of his new discoveries. From his epochal potato onwards he had been excellent newspaper copy, and while he complained about visitors and interviewers interrupting his work, he took pride in his huge scrapbooks of clippings. So well regarded was he by 1905 that the Carnegie Institution agreed to give him $10,000 a year (the equivalent of close to a quarter million today) to support his work. A botanist connected with the Institution would go to Santa Rosa to work with him, the idea being to pin down in scientific terms just how Burbank was performing his wizardry. Despite his standing as a scientist, a reputation eagerly claimed by the great man himself, he had never published details of his experiments.

The man dispatched to Santa Rosa was George Shull, an up-and-coming young experimental botanist already known for his genetic work. On and off over the next five or six years, Shull did his best to make sense out of Burbank's procedures. A report written after his first year, but never made public, resounds with frustration. He had trouble getting Burbank to give him interview time. The hybridiser's records were sketchy or non-existent, mostly kept in his head; there was often no available information about the original specimens before hybridization, leaving no basis for statistical study; the crossbreeding was done in a manner often slapdash at best. Shull, who clearly grew up in a different school, could scarcely conceal his horror as he described Burbank pollinating plants without ensuring against self-fertilization or keeping insects (and hence different pollen) away. Worst of all, Burbank had no respect for or interest in Mendelian genetics, and was firmly convinced that 'nothing but acquired characteristics could be inherited'. To Shull, who in a few years would be himself responsible for discovering hybrid corn, one of the most important discoveries in modern botanical science, Burbank's stubborn rejection of the best new thinking was next to heresy.

At the time, none of Shull's comments was published. They went straight into the Carnegie Institution files and apparently stayed there until long after Burbank's death. For reasons that are not altogether clear, the Institution ceased funding Burbank after five years (Burbank was furious – he had understood the grant period to be ten years). The comprehensive scientific report by Shull that Carnegie had projected never came out; instead Burbank stepped in by himself publishing a vast, bland twelve-volume account of his work. Aimed at a popular audience and heavily illustrated with photographs (unusually for the time, in colour), *Luther Burbank: His Methods and Discoveries and Their Practical Application* contained little analysis and no criticism at all. Not in the least rigorous or detailed, it served mainly to reinforce his reputation as the man who could make plants do anything.

Burbank died in 1926, reportedly a millionaire, and was buried near the greenhouse in his garden. By then doubts about the scientific quality of his work had begun to percolate more widely among botanists and geneticists and would increase as time went on. Not all of his discoveries proved satisfactory on other continents and in different climates. But among the general public there was only admiration. With enormous patience and endless labours he had, almost like some secular god, created dozens of new and improved plants – fruits, flowers, trees. Wizardry indeed.

Today his garden is a tourist attraction, drawing close to 100,000 visitors a year. In Santa Rosa, at least, he's famous. Whether or not he was really a scientist, or something approaching a transplanted

New England crank, may be irrelevant. Luther Burbank deserves
to be remembered, and probably will be – by me anyway.

A Galaxy of Gardeners

Britain hasn't always been a nation of gardeners. Three hundred years ago, according to Andrea Wulf, our gardens were pretty dreary places during a good part of the year, and even when things warmed up and the sun was shining, there wasn't much to look at except turf and topiary. What happened to change things is the subject of *Brother Gardeners*,[*] an engaging and authoritative trot through horticultural history that brings before us not only a splendid array of non-native plants ranging from paper birch to pelargoniums, but an equally splendid array of colourful, distinctly green-thumbed characters whose interest in botany generally bordered on the fanatic.

There was, for example, Philip Miller, possibly the most experienced horticulturist of his time, who virtually created the Chelsea Physic Garden in the fifty years he spent there, and for the first time offered detailed instructions for growing all manner of plants in his practical guide, *The Gardener's Dictionary* (1731). Miller was, moreover, a collector, determined to acquire as many new species as he could get from a wide network of foreign contacts, swapping or cajoling or – if absolutely necessary – purchasing seeds. Many of the most familiar and valued of our garden inhabitants were first flowered here by him.

If Philip Miller was the consummate professional plantsman,

[*] *The Brother Gardeners: Botany, Empire and the Birth of an Obsession* By Andrea Wulf (Heinemann)

Peter Collinson was the amateur, but on a no less effective level. A Quaker cloth merchant obsessed with collecting and cultivating unfamiliar varieties, he was the London end of an extraordinary double act that saw hundreds of new trees, shrubs, climbers and flowers introduced into Britain. Collinson's achievement, apart from his personal talents as a gardener (one of his tricks was to keep seagulls with clipped wings to eat snails and slugs), was to sponsor the work of a Philadelphia farmer and self-taught botanist named William Bartram, whom he encouraged to scour eastern America from the Carolinas to New York for new plants. The result was a flow of precious seeds for hitherto unknown species, many of which – exceptionally – were perfectly suited to the British climate.

Bartram eventually made a business of his collecting, packing up standardized boxes of seeds for dispatch to a number of rich English enthusiasts. One of his first subscribers was Lord Petre, owner of a thousand acres of parkland in Essex, and a tree-planter on a heroic scale. Petre created whole forests of American species and did much to break the mould of gardening style; in the wake of his plantings at Thorndon came the great era of eighteenth century landscape design and the heyday of 'Capability' Brown. First among the aristocracy and then gradually among Britons at large, a taste for gardening grew and grew. By mid-century it had even infiltrated fashion: when she turned up at court 'dressed in a white satin gown that was embroidered all over with trees, hills and flowers', writes Wulf, the Duchess of Queensberry 'was said to have looked like a walking landscape garden'.

Many people contributed to the boom. The Swedish botanist

Linnaeus with his new binomial system made sense out of the chaos of plant names; his one-time student Daniel Solander came to England to play a central role in encouraging botanical studies, and join the explorer, plant-hunter and scientific impresario Joseph Banks on his voyage of discovery to Australia. And Banks himself, founder of Kew and long-time president of the Royal Society, as plant-mad as any of them, devoted his energy and talents to making imperial Britain as great a botanical power as it was politically. The new plants kept coming. In the two decades following 1789, when the first edition of *Hortus Kewensis* was published, the number of species cultivated at the Royal Botanic Garden had increased from 5,600 to more than 11,000.

So with plenty of new species to play with, now reasonably priced thanks to the enterprise of nurserymen, a horticulturally friendly mild and wet climate, and the encouragement of fashion, Britons proceeded to make gardening the national art it still is. 'We have given the true model of gardening to the world', Horace Walpole could crow. 'Let other countries mimic or corrupt our taste; but let it reign here on its verdant throne'.

* * * * * * * * *

In 1733 a disgruntled but extremely rich Whig minister and one-time military man named Richard Temple, 1st Viscount Cobham, lost his political position and retired to his country estate in Buckinghamshire, thereby giving a whole new meaning to the expression 'gardening leave'. Because what Cobham undertook to complete in his exile from power was Stowe, the most celebrated and influential of all English landscape gardens. Representing the efforts over the course of some forty years of at least three of the premier designers of the era – Charles Bridgeman, William Kent and Brown – Stowe still survives (in rather diminished form, it has to be said) as a testament to the heights achieved by this most British of art forms.

In the judgement of Tim Richardson, that Cobham was a Whig, and a particular brand of anti-Walpolian Whig, is a matter of some significance. Though *The Arcadian Friends** is a history of the 'invention' of the English landscape garden during the closing years of the seventeenth century and the first half of the eighteenth, it is hardly a bucolic tale of trees and earthworks. On the contrary, the whole phenomenon appears to have had as much to do with politics as with parterres.

Admittedly, from the time of the Glorious Revolution in 1688 the British political scene was in extraordinary ferment. Among the tastemakers, the poets and the aristocrats and the newly rich, politics touched virtually everything. Party affiliations took shape around religion, around attitudes toward the royal succession, around historical differences, around public policy on such matters as war and finance. Under these circumstances, it may not be surprising that gardening – large-scale landscape gardening, anyway – was influenced too. One key reason for this is that gardens could and did function as a means of personal expression. By means of symbolism and allusions (say a statue of Hercules, referring to William III and the original Whig ideals), an estate owner might make a statement about his private beliefs – and possibly his political leanings.

Yet the progress of the landscape garden was anything but straightforward. The early Whig supporters of William of Orange

* *The Arcadian Friends: Inventing the English Landscape Garden.* By Tim Richardson (Bantam Press)

brought Dutch canals and topiary into their gardens (still to be seen in such restorations as Westbury Park in Gloucestershire), but designers also continued to draw on French and Italian styles, while Sir William Temple and Sir William Bentinck, both closely associated with the new monarch, introduced 'wiggles' – serpentine paths wandering through loosely planted woodland. Then there was Charles Howard, Duke of Carlisle, whose enormous Castle Howard and its gardens decisively domesticated landscape design as a British art form.

In a laudable if not entirely successful attempt to bring order to his history, Richardson's title implies that a group of like-minded designers, builders and estate owners was responsible for the creation of the landscape garden. That makes it sound simple. True enough, there were groupings like the famous Kit-Cat Club, a body of powerful Whigs (Carlisle was a key member) intent on seeing George I onto the throne, which also cared about gardening along with political intrigue, drinking, and business deals. Alexander Pope was certainly widely acquainted, with fellow gardeners among others, but his own famous garden by the Thames in Twickenham was absolutely idiosyncratic. Similarly Cobham, creator of Stowe, or Henry Hoare, whose later Stourhead remains an exquisite example of landscape art at its finest, achieved what they did mainly with the help of money and expert advice. This is not to minimize what they accomplished; it is just that it may be impossible in a single volume, even one as long and detailed and replete with first-rate scholarship as this, to make the narrative track. There were too many gardeners, too many gardens, too many disparate influences.

Even so, there are many delights here. Richardson's description of Pope's garden-making is excellent. I liked hearing about Jonathan Tyers, the owner of the London pleasure grounds Vauxhall Gardens, who went to the other extreme at his country estate by building a thoroughly morbid garden centred on a Temple of Death. And it is hard to forget the aristocratic landscape architect and proto-vegan Henry Herbert, 9th Earl of Pembroke, who decided to live on watercress and beetroot, nearly dying in the attempt. Whether he ever went back to meat or not is unclear, but he did survive to design a Palladian mansion for Queen Caroline and at least contemplate building a replica of Stonehenge on top of a hill at his estate of Wilton.

BOTANY

The Knotweed Challenge

The first time I laid eyes on Japanese knotweed, I thought it
looked pretty. Cascades of tiny white flowers, bright green heart-
shaped leaves, stately jointed stems rising nine feet or so over open,
uncluttered ground. Not so attractive in winter, perhaps, but you
could always cut the dead stalks and be assured that they would
emerge again in spring. I didn't know what to call it and figured it
must be some kind of bamboo. When we moved into an old house
in Western Massachusetts, it clustered around the venerable cedar
outside the front door, providing a nice counterpoint to the lilacs
on the other side.

I got a hint that there might be something fishy about my
bamboo around the time I learned its proper name. A plant
encyclopaedia told me it was properly called *Fallopia japonica* or
Polygonum japonicum or *Polygonum cuspidatum* or *Reynoutia japonica*
or – colloquially, with a note of horror – Japanese knotweed. The
'knot' referred to the bamboo-like nodes in the stem, but knotweed
had nothing to do with bamboo. There was a suggestion that it
might be a little tricky to control.

A patch grew next to the barn, and one autumn I decided to
replace it with mountain laurel (*Kalmia latifolia*). Somehow, the
knotweed's charm had run thin. It no longer looked pretty to me,
but uncomfortably alien. Its smell was a bit weird too (though
less so than privet). Mountain laurel, on the other hand, being

an authentic Berkshires native, certainly deserved the space more than knotweed did.

So I undertook to clear the ground. I chopped and dug and when I was done turned under some compost and a sprinkling of bone meal. The mountain laurel settled in happily enough. But a few months later what to my wondering eyes should appear, shooting up and through and over the cringing laurel, but an extremely vigorous, even manic copse of Japanese knotweed. My ground-clearing efforts had if anything made matters worse.

For years thereafter I tried to defeat that knotweed, and was still trying when the time came to leave New England for Old England. (The mountain laurel departed sooner.) I suspect it is still there, having achieved immortality. By then, in any case, it had my measure.

All this came to mind at 6:43 the other morning when, half asleep, I heard somebody on the *Today* programme say 'Japanese knotweed'. I later learned that some enterprising scientists believed they had found a way to tame the beast, by attacking it with a natural predator. Which is good, if not exactly fresh, news, since it has been obvious for a long time that without the fungi and insects that keep it humbled on the slopes of volcanic mountains in Japan whence it was exported some two hundred years ago, it was likely to go berserk. After all, it will thrive in nearly any moderately moist soil, even those poisoned by heavy metals, and has the capacity to generate a new plant from a piece of rhizome as small as an inch in less than six days. (The full-grown rhizomes, incidentally, may be 20 metres long and descend to a depth of 3 metres; I can testify from experience that they are virtually impossible to extract whole from the earth.) Few plants classed by gardeners as 'thugs' can approach the ability of knotweed to grow fast – four or five inches in a good day – and unstoppably – concrete or tarmac scarcely slow it down. So once you have Japanese knotweed, chances are you'll have it for a long time.

I don't doubt that the first plant hunters to introduce knotweed to the West, probably to Holland between 1820 and 1840 (it got to the UK in 1855), thought they were onto a good thing. They had no real reason to be suspicious. It soon became a popular ornamental and in the 1870s the well-known gardener-cleric Charles Wolley-Dod enthusiastically recommended planting it as a means of smothering nettles (it will). The even more distinguished William Robinson was also a fan, regarding it as 'most effective in flower in the autumn' and advised setting out in clumps of two or three for a nice effect (one would probably would have done the trick). Robinson did hint that there *was* a chance of knotweed 'overrunning other things' in the garden proper, although it could be 'very handsome indeed' along a stream or naturalised in a shrubbery.

Whether misguided attempts at naturalisation were responsible or knotweed's innate propensity to roam, it escaped from the confines of the garden. In Britain, where in 1900 only half a dozen wild growths were reported, by 1940 there were hundreds, and today they can be found in nearly every part of the country. (Only the Orkneys are knotweed-free – at the moment, anyway.) According to Richard Mabey's *Flora Britannica*, it now rejoices in the official title of Britain's most pernicious weed. The situation is no better in Europe, with wild stands thriving from southern

France and northern Italy to Norway, and in much of North America. One curious aspect of the situation is the fact that all the knotweed outside Japan is the clone of a single female, because it will reproduce only vegetatively.

Now it *is* possible to get rid of knotweed, but it isn't easy. According to one source, the cost could be as much as £9 a square metre. Other estimates put the total price of eradicating it from Britain at £1.56 billion. Repeated cutting over several years may slow it down, but you need to be very careful not to drop any fragments – they will take root. Some (very hungry) animals will graze it down, though grazing alone won't kill it. At the moment the most feasible method of controlling knotweed is the use of herbicides, although it is unfazed by most of them. Authorities recommend cutting the stem just below the first node, and injecting into it 10 ml of glyphosate made up ten times stronger than for normal application. If such a heroic procedure strikes you as excessive, believe me, it isn't; Japanese knotweed has a will to live virtually unmatched in the plant kingdom.

Given the cost and the attendant awkwardness of using herbicides, a good bit of effort has gone into the search for alternative control methods, which brings us to the announcement I heard on the radio. As it turns out the news isn't really news at all. The tiny sap-sucking psyllid jumping plant louse has been known for a long time to be a knotweed enemy. A native of Japan, it lays its eggs on the plant and the juvenile insects suck the knotweed's sap, killing it or at least making it seriously sick. This serves as a pretty effective control, presumably reducing the need for herbicides or (fruitless) digging, and just possibly bringing an end to the triffidish rampage of the knotweed.

According to an organization called Commonwealth Agricultural Bureaux International, which seems very keen to bring on the psyllids, extensive research has established that they won't eat anything other than knotweed. This is, of course, the key issue. The history of biological controls is littered with fiascos and disasters in which the Law of Unintended Consequences sometimes seems to reign supreme. The case of the cane toad, introduced into Australia in 1935 by sugar cane farmers battling beetles, is famous: the toads ate a few beetles and then went on eating practically anything that moved and was small enough; they also multiplied so fast that they are now hopping all over northeastern Australia. On the other hand, the wonderfully named moth *Cactoblastis cactorum*, which the Australians brought in to deal with another introduced pest, the prickly pear, did its job with efficiency and no untoward effects.

The scientists of CABI, who are incidentally funded by a consortium of major knotweed victims including Network Rail, the Cornwall County Council and the Welsh Assembly, are convinced – and convincing – about the safety of using psyllids in the UK. The insects' gustatory habits are so narrowly focused, they point out, that there is every likelihood that both the knotweed and the lice will expire at the same time – the one from attack, the other from hunger. They are also prepared to dismiss any sympathy for the target plant, which one expert regards as having 'the biodiversity value of concrete'.

So hope is in sight. A recent debate in the House of Lords, however, suggests that it may be too early to cheer. The red tape involved in getting clearance to introduce the psyllids is staggering. It might be simpler to get Osama bin Laden past Her Majesty's customs at Heathrow. Lord Hunt of Kings Heath, speaking for DEFRA, explained that it was first necessary to produce a 'pest risk assessment' and obtain a 'derogation' from European plant health legislation, after which there would be 'consultation with all stakeholders'. In the meantime, a peer review is being commissioned. 'My department', Lord Hunt assured the noble Lords 'is not at all complacent'. Which may on the whole be just as well, because there's nothing complacent about Japanese knotweed.

The GLP

Few flowers look quite as fake as a gold-laced polyanthus. Clustered atop a sturdy stalk, its blossoms (or 'pips') facing outward like so many little round plates, each of them comprising a bright gold centre ('eye') surrounded by a dozen or so deep red petals outlined by narrow gold 'wires', the GLP (as it is fondly known) gives the distinct impression of having been invented by a four-year-old, or possibly a seriously unskilled Sunday painter. It has charm, but of a startling, slightly unreal kind, as if it had turned up growing comfortably in a bed full of H. G. Wells's imaginary Martian plants.

The unreality is in fact real enough. The gold-laced polyanthus is a triumph of the plant breeder's art, a wholly artificial creation. Although its parentage has been traced to a cross between a red-flowered primrose brought from Turkey in the seventeenth century (*Primula vulgaris rubra*) and a hybrid oxlip (itself a cross between an English primrose (*P. vulgaris*) and a cowslip (*P. veris*), one thing fairly obvious in this fog of genes is that the marriage probably didn't happen accidentally. The polyanthus – and above all the gold-laced polyanthus that ultimately emerged after generations of pollen-dusted tinkering – was almost certainly the result of the efforts of gardeners. Moreover, it came into existence right here. Peter Coats, in his *Flowers in History*, goes so far as to single out the polyanthus as 'the only variety of flower which can be claimed as a purely British creation'.

I don't suppose I'd have ever paid much attention to the GLP, if I had not run across a book published nearly forty years ago by Roy Genders bearing the (to me) irresistible title of *Collecting Antique Plants*. Collecting flowers! What a wonderful idea – far more plausible than collecting rare books or Chinese paintings (both of which I have tried, not very successfully). All you need to do, according to Genders, is to search through old gardens looking for surviving specimens of plants that were thought to be extinct. 'In the same way', he writes, 'that the cottage home has maintained a constant supply of antique furniture, of china and glass and early English watercolours, so too, in the cottage garden are to be found many of the old fashioned flowers which also have antique value'.

Well, times have, as they say, changed. Unless it is owned as an upmarket second home (which it probably is), you won't find much antique furniture in a country cottage these days (to say nothing of 'early English watercolours'), while the cottage gardens are all in the Yellow Book and maintained by savagely knowledgeable plantspersons familiar with every growing thing right down to a buttercup. My chances of locating a rare plant in the lost gardens of Monmouthshire these days are vanishingly small, not least because of botanical ignorance. But when I got into Genders's book it soon became apparent that the 'collecting' part of his title was really a teaser for his true subject – the fascinating history of the old florists and their flowers, of the rise and sad fall of a whole horticultural civilization. Hunting for antique plants was merely a matter of truffling for surviving fragments of this mostly extinct world. And that is where we come back again to the gold-laced polyanthus.

Like most people who have ever given it any thought, I always held a rather Whiggish view of horticultural progress. That is, I assumed that developments in cross-breeding and the introduction of new varieties from abroad consistently led to improvements, and that improvements stayed with us. If a plant vanished it was probably because it was outclassed. I now realize that I was wrong. Witness the florists and their flowers.

The original 'florists' didn't sell flowers, they grew them, and they grew them competitively. Starting in the eighteenth century and continuing for hundred years or so, the term was used to refer to a group of amateurs who devoted themselves to breeding and growing a fairly narrow range of species: auriculas, hyacinths, anemones, ranuculus, certain tulips, pinks, carnations – and of course polyanthus. Their favourites tended to be those flowers you could grow in pots, in small back gardens. For the florists were mainly working men in pre-industrial towns and small cities, first and largely in the north, but gradually all over the country (apart from the southwest), whose home-centred occupations made it possible to keep a close eye on their plants all day long. Silkweavers working handlooms were one such group. Starting clubs, they organized shows, formulated rules and set about, with a concentration on horticultural minutiae difficult to credit, trying to outdo each other with prize-winning specimens.

It is clear that the pressure to compete brought extraordinary refinements to the chosen species, to none more than to the gold-laced polyanthus. Auriculas may have been less predictable, carnations and pinks more exotic (psychedelic even), but the GLP seems to have challenged devotees to heroic acts of potting-shed prowess. Special composts, some secret and some noisome, methods of watering, shading and careful temperature control – all these factors and more went into the process and were passed on like family treasures from one generation to the next. Above all in importance were the secrets of propagation and selection, because as time went on the specifications for a first-rate plant grew stricter and stricter. The stem had to be straight, strong and tall, with similarly rigid footstalks capable of holding the pips at the correct angle; each pip – there should be a minimum of five – had to be flat, smooth, and circular; the petal colour had to be dark crimson or red, with gold lacing running evenly around the edge of each petal without breaks or irregularities to the equally golden centre; the tube in the centre had to be perfectly round; the anthers had to be dense and curve inwards to hide the stigma completely. Serious failure on any point meant relegation to outer darkness, or at least ignominy for the contestant. Perfection, on the other hand, might mean the prize of a copper kettle.

Between 1760, when the first primitive GLP emerged, and 1860, when the fashion for it reached a peak and began to decline, hundreds of cultivars were developed. Some, like 'Bang Europe', sold for as much as a pound (nearly £75 today); most carried wonderful names: Barkess's 'Bonny Bess', Eckersley's 'Jolly Dragoon', Wilson's 'Bucephalas'. But the days of the local clubs were numbered. Though they didn't vanish completely – and new, hitherto beyond-the-pale plants like pansies and dahlias were admitted to their shows, largely because gardening had become a pastime for a wider public – the black smog of industrialization fell heavily across the florists' native home in the north, killing the plants and decimating the old social order. Gradually, the veteran growers died and were not replaced, and without their painstaking care the classic gold-laced polyanthus died out too. In 1971 Roy Genders could remark that 'most of the old florists' favourites have long since disappeared', hoping, nevertheless, that a few might still be found in cottage gardens. In 1936, though equally pessimistic, Sacheverell Sitwell thought it might be worth searching in Lancashire or Cheshire, or possibly around the village of Ironville, in Derbyshire, where in 1851 'this flower was the recreation of the miners'.

One place neither Genders nor Sitwell might have thought to look for something approximating the old GLP was France. Yet a mile or so from the sea on the north coast of Brittany can today be found a nursery with the unlikely (for France) name of Barnhaven Primroses. Among its exceptional offerings are a couple of gold-laced polyanthus, one red and one nearly black. How they got there is a story in itself, but the principal figure in the tale was responsible for preserving and developing so many great florist's plants that she might well be regarded as a latter-day florist herself.

Florence Bellis, nèe Hurtig, developed a passion for primroses before World War II, establishing Barnhaven Nursery in Oregon and making a name for herself as a breeder. Meanwhile in England, nearly all the old named varieties of GLP had been lost. In 1945, however, someone sent seeds of the few surviving unimpressive cultivars to Bellis. They had been salvaged by a grower from the wreckage of his bombed garden. She painstakingly improved them, selecting and hand pollinating over the course of many years, until she retired in 1966. At that point she sent her entire seed stock back to England, where Jared and Sylvia Sinclair set up Barnhaven *redivivus* in Cumbria and continued to introduce new plants. Since then the operation has passed through still more hands and settled at last in Brittany, where it is being run by Lynne and David Lawson. A completely respectable gold-laced polyanthus from Barnhaven will cost you a fiver. Whether it is correct enough to have won a prize in Ironville in 1835 must be open to doubt.

Whatever the ultimate fate of the GLP – and it is by no means certain, since according to at least one commentator the survival rate of post-war cultivars was 'disappointing', with a tendency to die after flowering – newer strains are still being selected. The newsletter of the Northern Section of the National Auricula and Primula Society recently noted that the plant 'seems to be making a comeback, with a number of members growing and showing them'. What's plain, however, is that this improbable little flower will never again enjoy the fame and attention it attracted when a perfect specimen could win you a copper kettle for your tea. And that strikes me as a pity.

The Maize Maze

One of the very few things I regret about moving from the US to Britain is that I am no longer able to grow sweetcorn. I've tried – at first there seemed to be no good reason why the relatively balmy climate of the Welsh Marches (as opposed to the brutal weather in Western Masschusetts) should prevent my producing a supply of my favorite vegetable, or for that matter my next favorite, tomatoes. But I soon learned that the problem is sun. There just isn't enough of it. Rain we've got, fertile soil we've got, but plain old hot sun, day after day, is only a vague pleasant recollection.

It is understandable that corn – or rather maize, which to avoid confusion I will henceforth call it – delights in sun. It comes from Mexico, a prodigiously sunny place. But there is something odder about its Mexican origins than just a love of light. Unlike most other plants on the face of the earth, maize is a purely human invention. There is no such thing as wild maize. It did not exist before humans began cultivating it and it would not survive today if farmers and gardeners did not sow it and protect it. Millions of people around the world, from South Africa to Northern Italy and much of Latin America, depend on it for food. Yet in the words of Mexican anthropologist Arturo Warman, maize is 'truly a human invention'. Its origins are a deep mystery that has only recently approached solution.

When the Spanish conquistadors arrived in Mexico in the early sixteenth century, they found that maize was the staple local food, supplemented by beans and other vegetables. It still is. Nobody seems to have asked where it came from; the assumption was that, like other domesticated foods such as wheat, there was an ancestral wild version still lurking somewhere in the botanically unexplored back country. But when in the twentieth century botanists started looking for this ur-maize, it simply wasn't there. The only thing remotely like maize – and it was so remote that botanists at first placed it in a different genus altogether – was a wild grass called teosinte.

Instead of a cob surrounded by many kernels in rows, the classical maize form, teosinte had only a narrow spike bearing fewer than a dozen hard triangular seeds. The seeds, moreover, tended to fall off easily (or 'shatter'), while maize kernels cling. On the whole, the resemblance between the two plants was slight indeed. Yet one fact suggested a relationship: maize and teosinte could hybridize. Unless they actually belonged not only to the same genus but to the same species this shouldn't be possible. Far from settling the matter, however, this just stirred up controversy, which would eventually become personal.

The idea that maize descended from teosinte was difficult to credit for several reasons. Standard evolutionary theory said that organisms develop from primitive to advanced and never the other way around. The covering (known as the glume) on maize kernels was soft, a primitive trait, while that of teosinte was hard – an advanced trait. Similarly, teosinte had single female spikelets (advanced) to maize's paired spikelets (primitive). And there was a more basic problem. Evolution customarily proceeds by small steps over long expanses of time. In this case intermediate forms were completely lacking – and so, in a crucial sense, was time. Maize could not develop by itself – its failure to drop seeds and other characteristics make its reproduction in the wild impossible. Humans were needed to plant and tend it, and to select better strains as they occurred. Yet the gap between the arrival of the first humans in the Western Hemisphere and the earliest examples of maize was no more than ten or twelve thousand years, far too little to account for such a radical change. Was teosinte the real solution to the riddle?

In 1938, two Harvard geneticists published a paper saying flatly that it wasn't. Instead, they proposed, maize had descended from a now-extinct wild maize plant. Teosinte, rather than being the patriarch, was itself a hybrid between the original wild maize and another genus of Mexican grass called *Tripsacum* (otherwise known as gamagrass). To prove their case, Paul Mangelsdorf and Robert Reeves managed to make a cross between modern maize and *Tripsacum*, though with some difficulty: they were forced to cut back the silk at the top of the maize cobs, apply large quantities of *Tripsacum* pollen, rescue the resulting embryos surgically and grow them on agar dishes in the lab. The resulting heroically achieved crosses, moreover, were sterile.

But the thesis was attractive. Mangelsdorf and Reeves also pinned down four main factors that distinguished maize from teosinte, and declared that they could all be traced back to 'infection' from *Tripsacum* germplasm. In other words, maize – with help from *Tripsacum* – was responsible for teosinte, not the other way around. The enormous diversity of modern maize varieties (hundreds of so-called 'landraces' exist in the Americas alone, from tiny popcorn ears to multicoloured giants) had been similarly touched off, they claimed, by the invasion of *Tripsacum* genes.

For the next thirty years, the Mangelsdorf-Reeves hypothesis ruled the roost. Most popular accounts followed it; even high school texts and children's books accepted that this is what had really happened. Among geneticists, however, doubts remained. One scientist in particular, having comprehensively objected to bringing *Tripsacum* into the picture, was George Beadle. As a student at Cornell in the early 1930s, he had become convinced that an annual form of Mexican teosinte belonged to the same species as maize. In 1939 he wrote a paper arguing that there was no reason to hunt for a missing extinct maize ancestor when all of the main factors differentiating teosinte and maize could be explained by simple gene mutations. Mangelsdorf and Reeves might have succeeded in producing a *Tripsacum*-maize hybrid by means of surgery and agar dishes, he pointed out, but such a thing could never have occurred in nature.

It was not until the late 1960s, however, that the battle between Mangelsdorf and Beadle was really joined. After a remarkable career in which he won a Nobel Prize (for work with fruit flies) and the presidency of the University of Chicago, Beadle turned back to the maize puzzle. By then archaeologists had entered the picture. Searching for evidence of early American agriculture, a team under Richard MacNeish scoured and excavated a series of dry caves in the Tehuacán Valley of Central Mexico and eventually found nearly 25 thousand tiny cobs of primitive maize – some fragmentary, many no bigger than the filter on a cigarette. MacNeish turned these over for study to Mangelsdorf who, unsurprisingly, concluded that they confirmed his *Tripsacum* thesis.

Now, in a burst of articles, reviews, and lectures, George Beadle went on the attack. He was sure that Mangelsdorf was wrong. To bolster his case he grew an entire field of teosinte-maize hybrids and counted the variations to show that only four or five genes appeared to be involved in the transition. Then he led a group of fellow botanists and geneticists to Mexico's Balsas River valley to search for hitherto overlooked teosinte mutants. They didn't find any, but did bring back a useful stock of research material.

Beadle and Mangelsdorf both rallied supporters as the debate grew more acrimonious. There were angry face-offs at several conferences. Mangelsdorf scornfully dismissed Beadle's teosinte thesis. A Beadle man (Hugh Iltis, a botanist otherwise renowned for having bred a square cob that wouldn't roll off the plate) pointed out that Mangelsdorf's precious ancient maize from Tehuacán was in fact identical to a fully domesticated form of popcorn from Argentina.

Gradually the tide turned in favour of Beadle, particularly as the era of molecular biology opened and it became possible to study chromosomes and genes and their inner workings via an understanding of DNA. Other geneticists and biologists like Barbara McClintock (another Nobel laureate) joined in. The relationship between teosinte and maize, despite their apparent differences, was too close to deny. Somehow, somewhere, a series of mutations must have taken place and been noticed by scavengers and proto-agriculturists 9,000 years ago.

It is still a bit hard to believe, and not everyone does. Mangelsdorf, who died in 1989, maintained a version of his thesis to the end. Then in 1995, rather to the dismay of those believing that the puzzle had been solved, a fresh theory entered the field. Mary Eubanks, a researcher working at Duke University, announced that she had successfully and repeatedly cross-bred *Tripsacum* with a type of perennial teosinte called *Zea diploperennis. Z. diploperennis*, now rare and surviving only in the remote highlands of western Mexico, had been unknown at the time of Mangelsdorf's desperate breeding attempts with *Tripsacum*. Eubanks discovered that unlike all the other teosintes (there are five species and a number of sub-species) *Z. diploperennis* bred readily with *Tripsacum*. The resulting hybrid, moreover, was fertile.

Initial reaction to Eubanks' announcement was hostile. She was accused of carelessness in handling her specimens, and charged with using the wrong pollen by mistake. 'They said', she recalls, 'that I just had teosinte that was contaminated with corn'. But she persisted. If her findings are confirmed, they can be best explained by one possibility: that teosinte was indeed a primary ancestor of maize, but that *Tripsacum* also contributed some genetic material. The combination could have occurred in nature since there is evidence that *Z. diploperennis* was formerly much more widespread in Mexico, and the plants probably grew together. Within the last few years, in fact, actual ancient examples of such hybrids have been reported. The assumption is that at some point accidental hybridization was followed either by an explosive mutation (what McClintock termed 'genomic shock'), or a series of lesser mutations painstakingly selected by early Mexican farmers to arrive at modern maize. Archaeologists now think that the whole process was extremely rapid, taking place over a century or less.

It may be that Eubanks has at last solved the maize mystery, although powerful arguments based on molecular analysis continue to challenge her findings. Establishing the ancestry of maize would be a satisfying achievement. Yet the game is more than an academic one. Eubanks claims to have mated some of her *Tripsacum*-teosinte hybrids with modern maize, thus introducing into the maize gene pool valuable characteristics such as resistance to a serious pest called corn rootworm and greater ability to withstand drought. There is even the possibility of a perennial form of maize that unlike all the present varieties would not have to be planted each year. Personally, I'm impressed. But I would be even happier if she turned her extremely green thumb to growing a new variety of sweet corn that would thrive without so much sun – or at least with the unfortunately limited amount that we are able to supply in the Marches of Wales.

Long Live the Seeds!

I have a big box of open, partly-emptied seed packets and I suspect I'm not alone in this. It seems like a terrible waste to throw unused seeds away – seeds aren't cheap, for one thing, and who wants to be wasteful these straitened days? Besides, I've frequently planted seeds left over from the year before that germinated perfectly well once they were in the ground. But the seed packets pile up, a few dated as much as three years back. Something will have to be done.

It would be nice to know for certain whether old seed is still good, without having to plant it to find out. Given the extreme heaviness of the soil in my garden and its reluctance to dry out to tillable condition, I can't afford to spend a few weeks of growing time experimenting with viability. (There have been times when I was still waiting impatiently for the earth to crumble as late as the middle of May.) As a result, I'll probably go out and buy yet another batch of fresh seeds – beans, lettuce, tomatoes, zucchini – just to be on the safe side. And end up with still more leftovers that may or may not be any good.

Theoretically, it should be possible to establish with reasonable certainty the likelihood of seed survival. While some touchy species bite the dust (perhaps not the best metaphor) almost as soon as they ripen, others are prepared to hang on for years, decades, even centuries. The other day I ran into a table listing in some detail the life expectancy of a large variety of vegetable and flower seeds ranging from salsify to physostegia, which I would dearly like to trust. Most vegetable seeds, it says, are supposed to be good for three to six years, with only parsnips and okra fading inside one to three. (Cantaloupe seeds, exceptionally, may still sprout after ten years, which recalls the tradition that melon seeds *need* to age; John Claudius Loudon's great *Encyclopedia of Gardening* (1835) suggested carrying them around in your pocket 'near the body' for a couple of months before planting. This was supposed to harden and mature them, though it's difficult to believe that any living object would be greatly improved by jostling small change and one's house keys over an extended period of time.) Flower seeds tend to be a good deal shorter-lived; apart from salpiglossis and nasturtiums (would you believe seven years?), they average two to four. Salvia, delphiniums, gerbera and a few others are good for only a year.

Whether any vegetable or flower seeds survive, of course, depends largely on the conditions under which they are kept. Certain large seeds and nuts (as well, of course, as the seeds of aquatic plants) cannot be dried and kept for replanting; an acorn, for example, normally falls to the ground and germinates in the same season, or it rots and can't germinate at all. Drying it doesn't preserve it, it kills it. But most seeds do become dormant with drying, ready to grow again with moisture, warmth, and light. To save them for later use the drying process must be gradual and complete, after which they should be kept cool – between freezing and about 5°C – in tightly sealed containers at moderate humidity – in the dark.

Needless to say, my half-empty seed packets have not received this kind of care and attention. The seeds they contain may or may not be defunct. But the subject of botanical longevity is a fascinating one, and in the case of *extreme* longevity a matter of legend and controversy. Some sensational claims have been made. The classic example is barley seeds that were found in the 3,000-year-old tomb of King Tutankhamun and reportedly germinated after planting. Even more wonderful are tales of viable arctic lupine seeds discovered in a lemming burrow in the Yukon and a ground squirrel nest in Alaska; geological data suggested that the animal holes were at least 10,000 years old. And there are more examples of botanical Methuselahs, including lotus seeds found in a sunken boat in Japan dating from 3,000 years ago.

According to the stunningly learned and authoritative *Seeds: Physiology and Germination* by J. D. Bewley and Michael Black, however, none of these claims are to be trusted. So far as the arctic lupines are concerned, nobody can prove that the seeds are as old as the burrows. King Tut's barley did not in fact germinate; it was 'extensively carbonised' and quite dead. And there is always a chance that the Japanese lotus seeds may have filtered into the boat along with other silt. The best candidate that Bewley and Black can come up with is a specimen of *Canna compacta* seed found – freakishly – *inside* a walnut in an ancient Argentinian cave. The seed had apparently been deliberately inserted into the immature nut in order to make a rattle; the nut ripened, hardened and dried with the seed inside. Carbon-dating of the nutshell established that it was about 600 years old, which meant that the canna seed – which successfully germinated – must have been the same age.

In practical terms, seed survival is probably less remarkable. Dependable examples of reasonably long life have been located among the seed collections dating back to the eighteenth century in London and Paris. A particularly nice one involves some seeds of the silk tree *Albizia julibrissin* sent from China in 1793 and lodged in the British Museum. In 1940 a German incendiary bomb dropped near the museum and in the course of quenching the flames the 150-year-old seeds got wet. They germinated. The staff planted out three seedlings and all went well until, a year later, another bomb fell and terminated the seedlings.

One of the most enduring attempts to solve the question of seed longevity may be credited to a pioneering plant scientist named William James Beal. Beal was an interesting man. Partly for geographical reasons I feel close to him – he was born in 1833 in Southern Michigan, my own home country, on what was then the frontier, not far from the place where, a hundred years later, my father would own a farm. Labouring, teaching, scrabbling for a proper education (he was over thirty before he finally received a science degree from Harvard), Beal eventually became the professor of botany and horticulture at the new Michigan Agricultural College (now Michigan State University). He spent the rest of his career there, teaching everything from plant physiology to landscape design to history, conducting research on breeding and forestry, creating a botanical garden (one of the first in America), and trying to establish exactly how long seeds – particularly weed seeds – could remain viable.

Beal cared about weeds because he cared about farmers, and farmers cared a lot about weeds. Before the days of glyphosate, all-too-healthy weed seeds posed real problems (and still do, for gardeners like me and you). They lurked in the soil, ready to spring into belated life as soon the ground was ploughed. It has been estimated that where an average of thirty-five weed seedlings might be found growing in a square metre of good earth, upwards of 780 would sprout from seeds hidden in newly-disturbed soil. So in 1879 Beal began what is now the longest-running scientific experiment in the world. On a sandy knoll in a secret location, he buried twenty bottles containing fifty freshly-harvested seeds each of twenty-one different kinds of plants, almost all weeds. (A few acorns and walnuts were buried too, not in bottles; they promptly rotted.) The seeds were mixed with damp sand taken, Beal explained, from three feet below the surface, 'where the land had never been ploughed', and the bottles were buried uncorked and mouth downward. This was intended to prevent water from accumulating and to allow normal gases to move around the seeds – natural conditions, in other words. Then, at five-year intervals, the bottles would be dug up one by one, and the seeds tested for viability.

William James Beal died ninety-one years ago but today five of his bottles continue to dream away underground in their still-secret tomb. In 1920 (a year having been skipped because of an untimely hard frost), it was decided to increase the interval to ten years to make the experiment last longer, and in 1980 further extended to twenty. This had a point, because there is one variety – the moth mullein *Verbascum blattaria* – whose seeds are still staving off oblivion and may well go on doing so for decades yet. In 2000, when the most recent bottle was unearthed, no less than 46% of the *V. blattaria* seeds deposited there 128 years ago germinated enthusiastically. A single seed of *Malva rotundifolia*, a mallow, also came to life, as did two examples of a species verbascum. Everything else had expired, most of them at least seventy years ago. Few annuals, in fact, made it to even five years.

Plainly, buried bottles are not the best way to keep seeds (except possibly verbascum). Far more serious challenges to extinction are the several large-scale seed banks that have got underway in the last few years. These involve humidity and temperature controlled chambers (including freezing vaults), facilities for propagating short-lived species, gene research and much else. The Millenium Seed Bank, run by Kew and funded in part by lottery money, aims to collect and preserve seeds from some 24,000 species of plants, among them all of the UK's native flora. In northern Norway, a still-larger seed bank blasted out of the permafrost is being filled with 4.5 million samples of food crop seeds from all over the world; they will be kept at a permanent -18 °C 'indefinitely'. Anyone interested in preventing the loss of precious species and their attendant genes will wish these enterprises luck. But they offer me no more than cold comfort when it comes to dealing with that pile of seed packets.

The Political Fly

'It is now become', the New Jersey gentleman farmer wrote with feeling, 'the most opprobrious Term our Language affords & the greatest affront our Chimney Sweepers and even our Slaves can give or receive, is to call or be called *Hessian*'. The year is 1788, the American Revolution is scarcely over, and colonials like George Morgan who won it are still smarting at the memory of the German mercenaries hired by the King to fight against them. But just now Morgan is not talking about the hated redcoats from Hesse. He is talking about an equally despised and feared invader to the new United States. He is talking about a fly.

Insect pests come and go. Farmers contend with them every day, now perhaps more efficiently (and lethally) than in the past. With our sprays and drenches and *bacillus thuringiensis*, even we gardeners don't get terribly worked up over insects. That national governments should do so seems improbable in the extreme, but the Hessian fly was clearly a special case. Looking back, it seems safe to say that few insects in history can have been responsible for such an international furore.

What's known today by the sinister name of *Mayetiola destructor* is in fact a tiny gall midge of the order *Diptera*, rather frail and harmless in its adult form. As a larva, however, hatched from eggs laid on the stems of wheat and other grain, it is a voracious creature. It will bore in, preventing the development of multiple stems and causing the plant to collapse. The result may well leave a field looking, as one despairing farmer put it, 'like a herd of cattle had passed through it'.

George Morgan, along with many of his fellow farmers, was convinced that the fly had actually arrived in America from Europe together with the Hessian troops in 1776, carried on wheat straw used as forage for their horses. According to the late Phillip Pauly, whose exhaustive study of the Hessian fly saga considers various possibilities, this theory may well be true, although the facts remain murky. The fly had never been reported in the Old World, and it was hitherto unknown in the New. What's certain is that it began turning up in New York, New Jersey and Connecticut during the late 1770s and the 1780s, attracting excited and appalled attention from the best and the brightest of the fledgling nation. Scientists, politicians and farmers (some men, like Thomas Jefferson, were all three) corresponded about it and learned societies published reports. Governor George Clinton of New York opened the state legislature session with a speech calling attention to the crisis and asking that remedies be shared. The situation was desperate. 'We could combat their other Hessian Auxiliaries', a friend wrote George Washington, 'but this is unconquerable'. A general alarm spread among those whose livelihood depended on harvesting wheat – and exporting it.

In the years following the Revolution, the infant United States was concerned not only with developing a new political system, but with building an economy. Inevitably, this was agriculture-based and to considerable extent dependent on shipping such products as cotton and grain to Europe. Britain especially was a prime market. But if the Hessian fly posed a threat to wheat ripening in the fields of Long Island and Princeton, it soon took on an ominous new and quite unexpected role.

In the spring of 1788, the British consul in Philadelphia, a dubious character called Phineas Bond, learned that American merchants were preparing to ship a large quantity of wheat to England. At this point the British government was in the hands of a group of aristocratic politicians thoroughly soured by the loss of the colonies and perfectly unsympathetic with the idea of any kind of trade with the new country. As landowners themselves, moreover, they stood to gain by a rise in the price of wheat in Britain, if the Philadelphia shipment could be banned. Bond gave them the perfect excuse: the Hessian fly. The wheat should be excluded on the grounds that it could carry the fly and infect British fields. Consulting their scientific adviser, the eminent polymath Sir Joseph Banks, the Privy Council promptly agreed and George III (then approaching his first bout of madness) signed off on the prohibition. No more American wheat.

Banks, while enough of hard-liner to agree with the ban in any case, was also a scientist who realised that so far as the Hessian fly was concerned, he was flying blind. He had never seen one, and had only a name and a vague description to go by. Yet if this creature was as dangerous as it seemed to be, it was, in his words, 'an Evil of a most dreadful Nature'. He began investigating.

Meanwhile, American reaction was predictable. In his initial reaction, Banks had confused the Hessian fly with another wheat pest, the Virginian 'wevil'; one angry American pointed out that the two 'were as different as a Toad from a Snake'. Jefferson, in

Paris, complained of 'a libel on our wheat'. The revolutionary polemicist Tom Paine declared outright that the whole gambit was simply a dodge to benefit British farming interests, i.e. the gentlemen running the country. And the Duke of Grafton, in his lordly wisdom, opined that the Hessian fly was nothing less than a heavenly judgment 'upon such ungrateful colonies and rebellious people' as the Americans, who deserved to suffer.

Banks completed his investigation by February 1789. By now he could claim to know as much about the Hessian fly 'as the Americans themselves', but having straightened out the entomology he nevertheless chose to exercise caution. Without 'positive proof that no danger whatever exists' (clearly impossible) the prohibition would stand. The price of wheat in Britain rose inexorably.

American concern, however, was strangely muted. Britain, it turned out, was not the only market for wheat. A bad European harvest had caused serious shortfalls. A doubling in the price of bread in France, famously reflected in Marie Antoinette's recommendation of cake, exacerbated the rising spirit of revolution there. In England the government, beset by King George's now full-blown madness and the threat of popular unrest on the French model, began to view the swelling price of wheat in a less positive way. By the end of 1789, with incipient starvation in some parts of Britain and much talk of revolution, the terrifying prospect of an insect plague somehow faded in importance. The potential for infection from France, as Pauly says, suddenly seemed greater than infection by the Hessian fly. The nervous Privy Council had second thoughts about the ban. A query went from London to the British agents in America:

was it not true that the Hessian fly hazard had abated? And was there possibly wheat available at a good price? Then, without even waiting for an answer, the embargo was lifted.

Ironically, the Hessian fly hazard had not abated; it was, if anything, as devastating in the United States and – eventually – Canada as it ever had been. But the resumed shipments of grain never carried the pest to England. There was no way that they could; the Hessian fly did not attack threshed wheat but only the leaves and stems of growing plants. There had been no real danger.

In the fields of America, however, the threat never went away. Some northern farmers in Connecticut and New Jersey gave up on wheat altogether. All during the nineteenth century, as settlements and new farms moved west across the continent, the fly moved with them, periodically causing crises. In 1836, for example, a severe infestation bankrupted many wheat growers and helped create the financial Panic of 1837. Agricultural experts devoted whole libraries of studies to the bug. Employing decoy crops, better agricultural techniques, different wheat varieties ('yellow bearded' wheat proved less susceptible, but produced a lower-quality flour) and, most successful, delaying planting until after the egg-laying season (the 'fly-free' date), farmers gradually learned to contend. They still need to. Because today, more than two hundred years after the presumed arrival of *Mayetiola destructor* with the Hessian mercenaries in New York, its descendants continue to flutter around the grain fields of North America, waiting to pounce.

Names

Around two thousand years ago, a Greek doctor named Dioscorides described a plant that he considered to be medically useful. It was called 'crocodilium', he said, and it was supposed to help people who were splenetic. When boiled and drunk, it 'causes copious bleeding at the nose'. Other characteristics, apart from the shape of its roots and seeds, and the fact that it grew in 'wooded places', were unfortunately obscure.

What exactly *was* crocodilium? And why should anyone care? As Anna Pavord splendidly makes plain in this elegant and scholarly history of taxonomy,* a science usually regarded as even gloomier than economics, such questions are far from insignificant. Exactly which plant is which, and its relationship to other plants, are matters central to our understanding of the world we live in. Crocodilium is a case in point, though on the whole a depressing one. The confusion surrounding it, as with so many of the plants mentioned by Discorides, lasted for hundreds and hundreds of years. Even when the sixteenth century Italian botanist Luca Ghini finally managed to pin it down as being most likely a species of eryngium (at the same time apologizing for not drinking an infusion to see whether it really did make his nose bleed), he was taking only a modest step out of the chaos.

In Pavord's firmly expressed view, the problem started with the ancient assumption that plants should be viewed primarily

* *The Naming of Names* By Anna Pavord (Bloomsbury)

in terms of their usefulness. In practice, this meant their use in medicine. Right up until – and throughout – the Renaissance, botanical studies concentrated on pharmacology, ignoring what she calls 'the big picture, the altruistic, intellectual search for the key to the order of the universe'. What was interesting about clove pinks was their efficacy against the plague, not their flowers or the genus they belonged to.

Yet from the very beginning, in the work of the often-overlooked third century B. C. Greek philosopher and proto-botanist Theophrastus, another approach could be discerned. Theophrastus is one of Pavord's heroes, and rightly so. The first man to write a book about plants, his 'complex, quizzical take' led him beyond mere recording to think about plant relationships, about names, about the actual shape of the natural world and the way living things fit into it. Unfortunately, his works were lost in the West; they survived only among Arab scholars in the East. Dioscorides, the medicine man (and far less important figure), held sway in Europe, repeatedly translated, the one and greatest authority right up until the seventeenth century.

So most writing on plants took the form of herbals, simple lists of plants together with their therapeutic qualities. Despite advances in technology during the Renaissance – in engraving, printing, papermaking – that brought huge improvements in the way plants could be described, the old-fashioned herbal continued supreme. Gradually, however, the constant recourse to classical authority became harder and harder to justify. Northern Europe had plants that ancient Greeks could not have known (and vice versa); still more new species were flooding in from the Near East and the Americas. Instead of simply copying precedent, men like Otto Brunfels, Leonhart Fuchs, Ghini, and Andrea Cesalpino were inspired to make their own observations and develop their own techniques, such as creating herbaria of dried specimens. They also began to think about how plants might be related to each other. 'All science', wrote Cesalpino, 'consists in the gathering together of things that are alike'. In support of this thesis, he set out 1,500 plants in his own 1583 book *De Plantis* in thirty two different groups ranging from *Umbelliferae* to *Compositae*.

Cesalpino used similarities between fruits and seeds to classify his plants; Lobelius attempted to do the same using leaf shape in his '*nieuwe ordenighe*' of 1581. Neither worked very well. (Lobelius concluded that using it there was no way to distinguish apples from pears.) The Englishman John Ray, following the fundamental division into trees, shrubs, sub-shrubs and herbs first employed by Theophrastus, developed yet another more sophisticated classification scheme and got a little further. Yet there were always ambiguities or plants that didn't fit. Even today, it seems, serious classification problems remain.

Pavord writes delightfully about all this. Fine anecdotes and memorable pocket biographies tumble through what in lesser hands could be very dry text. Especially affecting is her account of the sad life of another of her particular heroes, the thoroughly forgotten churchman botanist William Turner. Turner, who seems to have been a sort of reverse Vicar of Bray, had the misfortune to be a committed Lutheran during the English Reformation. He was as bitterly opposed to the corruption of the Church of England under Henry VIII as he was to Catholicism under Queen Mary, and consequently spent a good bit of his life under both regimes in exile. When he was not abroad, he devoted himself to writing tracts, to securing a place (he was eventually appointed Dean of Wells, but couldn't get his predecessor to vacate the position), and, above all, to collecting and studying plants. He had a hard time of it; at one point he pleads that his 'chylder' had been 'fed so long with hope that they ar very leane'. But he still succeeded in producing what Pavord calls 'the first decent plant book' in English, the *New Herball* (1551, 1568). This might have been a triumph, except for the fact that the first part was banned because of his over-energetic Protestantism, while the second part was published in Germany where nobody could read English.

While Turner's problem may have been unique, it is certainly true to say that language has played an extraordinary part in the history of taxonomy. Giving distinctive labels to plants has never been a straightforward matter, because classification and naming have to go together. Without a system incorporating relationships – families, genera, species – a binomial name of the kind established by Linnaeus can't exist. There have been many times in the past when the whole naming process seemed likely to crash. Common names could vary from place to place. Or a plant might be lumbered with half a dozen Latin terms to identify it. And simpler names could be dangerous or confusing. As Thomas Johnson (c.1600-1644), another of Pavord's heroes for his ground-breaking exploration of native British flora, pointed out, herb-women in London often sold the easy-to-find hemlock water dropwort in place of water lovage, just by changing the name. Water dropwort is poisonous.

If I have any complaint to make about *The Naming of Names*, it is to wish that it were longer. I would have liked to hear more about the struggles of scientists since the eighteenth century to refine the taxonomic structure, which are apparently still going on. What changes lie in store? Will chrysanthemums be relegated to outer darkness again on the strength of their DNA? What about geraniums? In any event, with the case Pavord makes for Theophrastus, I trust the namers will now memorialize him, with a genus of his own at the very least.

COUNTRY LIFE

Wild West Wind

I never used to worry much about wind. In my experience an occasional disemboweled umbrella or an eyeful of dust was about the worst of it. I've been on the edge of a typhoon without too much discomfiture and I faintly remember a tornado passing through Southern Michigan when I was seven or eight, but on the whole I don't harbour many negative feelings about a good sharp breeze. After all, I enjoy flying kites and sailing dinghies, neither of which occupations (whatever else you may think of them) are in the least entertaining in a flat calm. The storms this year, however, have given me pause for thought.

Our old stone house in the Welsh Marches is on a rising ridge line facing southwest. Between us and the Bristol Channel is nothing but air – a few inadequate hills and the odd copse do practically nothing to break the flow that funnels up the estuary toward us. To the northeast the land falls away too, but on this side there is a small piece of woodland belonging to a neighbour and containing a number of big ash trees. In theory, these trees should shelter us when the wind comes from that direction, but in reality they simply sway alarmingly and behave as though they are getting ready to topple directly across the lane and onto our garden. (Or onto the house – I haven't worked out their exact height yet. I don't really want to know.)

But it is from the southwest that the wind truly counts. 80%

of the time it blows from that direction, generally following one of those doom-laden weather predictions on the ten-o'clock news filled with isobars and loose talk of the Beaufort Scale. What you notice first is a deep soughing noise, then an increasingly hysterical shriek as the gusts pick up speed and seem to batter the house. The hullabaloo is frightening, to be honest. If the wind is accompanied by rain – and it usually is – the battering is literal: a sharp rattle like bullets against (and sometimes through) the windows. This is the time to put on rain gear and go out and move the car out of the way of the half dozen large firs growing just beyond the parking area.

I began taking this precaution on a hunch last autumn, when I noticed one tree swaying in a particularly marked fashion. Having moved the car in the evening, the first thing I saw next morning was the tree, a full 16 inches through at the base, lying directly across the place where the car had been parked. Its top was just short of the bay hedge. Once I had cut it up with my chain saw and split it, the result was a considerable amount of not-very-good fireplace logs. (Fir, in case you are unfamiliar with it, explodes when it burns; even seasoned wood sparks dangerously.)

Trees falling in the wind have been a constant feature of life at Towerhill Cottage. We have a small wood – perhaps an acre – which when we arrived twenty years ago was largely filled with larches. They had been planted, presumably for timber, just after the war, and by the time I took them on they were facing defeat in their lifelong battle against the wind. During nearly every storm another one lost its grip on the earth, generally becoming awkwardly caught up high in another tree instead of falling to the ground. (One afternoon, reaching the house in the midst of a gale, I actually saw one go down, just keel over slowly as wind whipped its branches.) It is extremely difficult to saw up a hanging tree; for good reason lumberjacks in Michigan in the old days used to call them widow-makers. After trying this a few times, and getting the chain saw hopelessly jammed more than once, I thought better of the matter and called up Tony Heming the tree man. In the space of a week he and his crew felled the whole lot, dragged out the timber to be converted into garden fencing, burned and chipped the slash, and left me with an open, if be-stumped, meadow fit for grazing sheep and producing swathes of bluebells in the spring. Of course there were also a number of remaining big broadleaves – an avenue of oak and a scattering ash trees – that I chose to keep, and along the fence-line a large complement of dead or dying elms that I didn't. It is these, victims of the ubiquitous Dutch Elm Disease, that are now the wind's target. Cutting them up is not difficult, but splitting the chunks is the very devil, even with my otherwise sovereign heavy wedge-shaped splitting maul.

Gardening in the teeth of wind, including intermittent wind of the kind we have, is usually regarded as a matter of planning and windbreaks. Horizontal daffodils and shuddering clumps of wild windflowers may be okay, but horticultural manuals are forever telling you that many plants simply can't put up with such conditions. Frankly, I'm not altogether convinced. Several now-huge camellias face the wind with apparent insouciance. A *Taihaku* flowering cherry tends to lean to the northeast, but otherwise seems happy. Even the apricot planted in a tub on the terrace, prey to the worst the wind has to offer, obediently bears fruit.

Nevertheless, from the beginning we recognized that we ought to organize some serious windbreaks. Fortunately a preceding owner of Towerhill Cottage had planted a bay hedge; we found pieces of it struggling for survival but over the years were able it to restore to healthy plumpness. (Ironically, bay (*Lauris nobilis*) is usually not recommended as a windbreak; a famous gardening writer who came to visit went so far as to tell me that our hedge was horticulturally impossible. But it too is perfectly happy, and furnishes us with an unlimited supply of bay leaves for cooking.)

My largest enterprise in the way of windbreaks was to plant a beech hedge. This appeared straightforward enough until I realized that the windbreak would need to be protected by its own windbreak if it had any hope of maturing. So for a period of three or four years I was forced to erect – and re-erect whenever it blew down – a singularly ugly curtain of green perforated plastic designed to protect the infant beeches. This eventually worked; we now have about thirty feet of six-foot-high beech hedge which, as promised, holds its brown leaves right through the winter. It isn't really very attractive. But it certainly breaks the wind.

I have often considered planting some proper yew hedges, especially to replace the lonicera nitida I once put in as a stopgap. There is much to be said for lonicera – it grows fast, is wonderfully dense and compact, can be (indeed *must* be) sheared regularly. It also slows the wind, though given its tendency to tilt drunkenly under a heavy weight of snow, I'm not prepared to term it a true windbreak. Yew would certainly be preferable, if only because it wouldn't have to be cut so often.

As I write this, I can hear the wind beginning to rise. Luckily, it's still early spring and the trees haven't leafed out yet; the wind can't get a firm grip. But the weather report is calling for gusts of up to sixty miles an hour and I'm not too sure about a couple of those firs. The chain saw is sharp. But maybe I'd better go move the car.

Commuting with Cats

In 1898, the English town planner Ebeneezer Howard produced a neat piece of propaganda in support of his idea for 'garden cities'. It was a diagram listing disadvantages of life in town ('slums and gin palaces, foul air, isolation of crowds'), and the country ('lack of society, lack of amusement, lack of drainage'). Howard's proposed solution was the 'garden city', offering the best of both worlds.

For more than forty years I've been trying to reconcile city and country in my own way – that is, by travelling a perfectly ridiculous distance every weekend between two houses, one urban and one rural, first in America and now in England. The trip isn't all that hard – I mean it's not exactly a trip across Death Valley with a small fries and a Diet Coke – although I've known those who like to paint it that way, with graphic descriptions of roadworks, traffic jams and vomiting infants. In my case, most of the perils of weekend commuting come down to one basic item: cats.

Some people are dog people. I prefer cats. Dogs are tough to manage during the week in the city – they have to be walked and all that, and they get neurotic if they are left alone by themselves. Cats don't have to be walked and they are pretty neurotic to start with (in a charming way, of course). The main difficulty with cats is to find them when you want them, and so far as commuting with cats is concerned, when you are ready to leave for the country or come back to the city, believe me, you want them.

When I worked in Manhattan, we lived in an apartment in Greenwich Village. The country house was in the Berkshire Hills of Western Massachusetts, about 130 miles away. The cats – we had two, Annie and Cleo – loved it up there. In the city they were kept indoors (New York is distinctly inhospitable to wandering cats), but in the country they could go outside whenever they wanted to. There were plenty of small animals to catch in the meadow, and not much competition from other cats. But if they enjoyed the country, they certainly didn't enjoy getting there. They devoted a great deal of ingenuity to finding new hiding places in the apartment when they sensed that the car was about to be loaded. Annie even figured out how to get *inside* the box spring of our bed, thus delaying our departure for half an hour one infuriating day. (The trick didn't work a second time.)

Annie was the elder of the two cats, and when we first got her, and decided to try taking her with us to the country, I built a huge travelling cage for her out of chickenwire and pieces of wood. It was big enough to hold a litter tray, water and food, as well as a blanket for her to lie down on. A regular hotel, and a serious mistake. Placed in it, Annie went berserk, squalling and climbing the side, tipping over the litter tray and spilling the water. I finally calmed her down by draping her blanket over the whole affair, creating a sort of damp cave that she could sleep in. I wish I could say that my next smart idea – taking her out on a leash halfway to Massachusetts to relieve herself – was equally successful, but as one of P.G. Wodehouse's characters sagely observed, cats are not dogs. It took me a while to learn this great truth.

Annie's cage occupied about a third of the floor space in our aging estate car. The rest was devoted to children baggage, groceries, bits of horse tack and other impedimenta. So when we acquired Cleo, our second cat, measures had to be taken. The first thing was to reduce the cage by half with a saw and wire-snips, and to buy a cat carrier for Cleo. This arrangement worked for a while, until the children thoughtlessly insisted on growing bigger. Eventually, with the cage replaced by another cat-carrier, a slightly larger estate car, and considerable forbearance on the part of all concerned, the trip became almost routine, or as routine as moving house twice a week ever could be.

In Greenwich Village, locating cats in preparation for the trip north was (provided you could think like a cat) relatively easy. After all, they had to be *somewhere* in those few smallish rooms, even if it happened to be inside a bed. Preparing to come back south on a Sunday afternoon was a different matter. As I recall, Cleo was fairly cooperative; you could usually count on her lazing around the back porch chewing on a vole or simply sleeping, and she seemed to lack the initiative to flee the dreaded cat-carrier. Annie was more enterprising. With unlimited space to hide in, and every incentive to avoid the trip to the city, she generally disappeared. If you allowed a certain amount of time (say an hour of so), you could – probably – find her. She was never actually left behind, though in retrospect it's hard to see why.

These days we make a similar trip, from London to a cottage on the Welsh border. The distance is the same, and the time it takes identical. In some ways our current cats, Rosie and Sam, are easier to handle. As brother and sister, they are willing to travel in the same cat-carrier, so space isn't a problem. And they both have phenomenal bladder control, useful when wrecks on the motorway or torrential English rain stretch out our time in the car to four or five hours. But the commute still has its awkward moments.

The main one is, as usual, making sure you've got the cats when you want them. Unlike Annie and Cleo in New York, Sam and Rosie in London are allowed to come and go through a cat-flap into the back garden whenever they want to, day and night. Consequently they have stopped using the indoor litter tray, and instead insist on using our garden (or a neighbour's – I haven't investigated) whenever nature calls. Fair enough. But think: this means that they must be allowed to go outside for a therapeutic drain not too long before they are placed in the cat-carrier. They can't be locked in the house the whole night before departure, just so you know they are available. On the other hand, if you let them go outside for a whizz, there's nothing to stop them heading straight over the garden wall into oblivion.

I apologize for going into such sordid detail; travelling with cats demands it. Fortunately, there are two sides to the availability conundrum, or rather two ends to a cat. They get hungry. And hunger has proved to be solution – at least so far.

Right up until breakfast time (which no right-thinking cat would miss) you leave the cat-flap unlocked, so they are free to use the facilities before returning indoors for their Friskies. While they are eating breakfast you lock the flap, trapping them, preferably in one or two rooms (in the country one, definitely, ever since Sam disappeared into an attic crawl space and stayed there until mid-afternoon). We usually leave at noon on Friday and return to the

Logs

An extraordinary story in the *Times* the other day recounted what's been happening to some venerable trees in Poole. Now Poole is a seaside town, and people who live beside the sea for some reason enjoy looking at it. (Being an inland person, I have no such predilection.) The problem seems to be that the trees got in the way of the sea views or, worse, occupied land that houses or flats with sea views might be built upon. Miscreants, mostly unidentified, were sneaking around topping trees, hacking off branches, girdling trunks, surreptitiously chopping through roots and even poisoning them. One man was fined £7,500 for pouring Jeyes fluid into the ground around an ancient pine for a year until it gave up the ghost. Another dug a hole next to an oak and dumped 25 pounds of rock salt into it. No word of the tree's reaction but one can guess.

Trees have been in the news a lot lately, generally as the subjects of man's inhumanity to nature. Trees are the good guys. There was a time, of course, when pioneers in the American wilderness felt differently – they couldn't wait to clear the woods so as to be able to see the sun, even if it meant living afterwards in something resembling a blasted heath. And Germany's Black Forest always had the reputation of a place more congenial to witches and goblins than tree-huggers. But nowadays, since the excitement over global warming, trees seem to be everybody's favourite plants. While I have no immediate objection to this point of view, it strikes me that it could do with a bit of deconstruction.

In the last few years my own closest involvement with trees has lain in felling them, chunking them with a chainsaw, and splitting them up for firewood. We burn a lot of firewood, driven by a combination of aesthetics and a need for heat. (Obviously we don't need heat in August, but I've seldom missed building a fire then anyway; it's psychologically warming.) I also burn – in bonfires – a considerable amount of slash from the tops of trees, branches and twigs and ivy that are too spindly to get rid of any other way. I don't have a chipper, though I'd like to; it has always seemed to me one step too far given the cost, the petrol, the noise, etc. But I'm troubled by all this incineration, and not certain whether or not I should be.

The question always circles back to carbon. I have tried to inform myself about climate change, and as I get it the main focus of concern is the amount of carbon, in the form of carbon dioxide, we are expelling into the atmosphere, largely through burning things like coal, oil and, yes, wood. (Of course there are other gases also helping to lay the heat-retaining blanket across the earth, like methane, but since we are talking about trees just now let's stick to carbon dioxide.) Like all plants trees make use of carbon dioxide in the process of photosynthesis, absorbing it and retaining it in its growing leaves, bark and other tissues. Scientists figure that about half of the dry weight of a tree consists of carbon. Every living tree locks up a certain quantity of it, and the more the atmospheric carbon dioxide it has to work with, the happier the tree. One study recently showed, in fact, that trees have been growing perceptibly bigger and faster since we began adding more CO_2 to the air. The average hectare of rainforest trees is consequently now soaking up 0.6 of a ton of carbon dioxide more than it did in the 1960s. And – in theory – so long as a tree is alive, the carbon dioxide can't get back into the atmosphere again.

But this where serious problems begin to arise, problems that tend to queer many of our assumptions about the infinite virtues of trees as carbon sinks. A 'carbon sink' is a feature, living or otherwise, that ties up carbon so it can't get into the atmosphere in the form of carbon dioxide. Examples of effective carbon sinks are coal and oil deposits or peat lands; such so-called fossil fuels hold the carbon permanently until human beings are foolish enough to burn them. We've been doing this at an increasing rate for two or three hundred years, which is exactly why we are in trouble with the climate today.

Unfortunately, while trees hold carbon too, particularly when they are growing, they also give it off through a process called respiration. This happens when the material created by photosynthesis begins to break down. What was a carbon sink then becomes, willy-nilly, a carbon source, more marked at night, even more marked in winter than summer. Eventually, with the death and dissolution of the tree, *all* the carbon goes back into the atmosphere. Still, it takes time. Broadly speaking, it may take fifty years for the average tree to move from being a sink to a source. This means that a tree planted now could do good work tying up carbon dioxide for quite a while, during which time we might be able to puzzle out some other solution for our overheating planet. Of course respiration increases with rising temperatures, which further confuses matters. Meanwhile an existing old forest is probably already giving off at least as much carbon as it is swallowing.

The argument for creating new forests is nevertheless a pretty good one. The UK government certainly thinks so. The Forestry Commission has proposed planting no less than 23,000 hectares a year for the next forty years. (This appears to be a staggering figure until you compare it with the amount of Amazonian rainforest being destroyed every year: roughly ten thousand times as much.) We are also told to plant trees in our gardens, or wherever else they might grow happily. If you are as beset with ash seedlings as I am, that ought not to be a problem, unless for some reason you object to trees in the herbaceous border.

I remain concerned about stoking my two fireplaces. We have a couple of acres of woodlot, out of which it is possible, given adequate muscle power, to extract enough logs to feed both of them. Most of what I cut is standing deadwood, smallish elms that have succumbed to disease, plus a motley mixture of ancient thorn and hazel hedging that has fallen into the sheep meadow, birch, ash and some larch. Because a given tree is no longer alive, it is certainly not absorbing any more carbon, and if it falls to the ground it will start decaying and become a carbon source. When I burn it, surely enough, the carbon will go straight up the chimney into the atmosphere, as if no tree had ever existed. The same goes for the bonfires – chipping the slash and letting it rot down (which, frankly, I'd prefer, because I could find use for the woodchips in the garden) also releases the carbon. On the other hand, for the last, say, thirty years that scruffy recently-deceased elm was most likely contributing to the well-being of the planet. Moreover, trees are renewable (remember those ash seedlings) and the alternative to burning them for heat would be to burn gas, a non-renewable fossil fuel. Fossil fuels contain in concentrated form the carbon accumulated over millions of years, securely locked up. The tree gives up only what it collected in its own lifetime.

The most valuable tree in Britain, I'm told, is a London plane in Berkeley Square. It's supposed to be worth £750,000, which seems a bit steep even for Mayfair. But it's still growing, so from a purely utilitarian point of view it must be worth a bob or two for carbon retention if nothing else. It is a very big tree. Needless to say I have nothing comparable in my woodlot. What I do have, however, is an abundance of acceptable firewood, plenty of saplings, and – as springtime makes evident – photosynthesis galore. On balance, I believe I'll go with the logs.

Critters

I've never had a particularly happy relationship with wild animals. Few gardeners have. The basic reason, of course, is that animals eat things we would sooner they didn't, and tend to make a mess in other ways when they are not hungry. Consider, for example, the natural habits of moles, which when they are not tunnelling shallowly in long runs just below the surface (into which one can easily slip and break an ankle), they are plummeting into the depths in search of earthworms and heaving up equally lethal hillocks of earth all over the lawn. For many years I have fought a running war with moles, first with 'mole smokes' (alas no longer available), then with mothballs, paraffin, exhaust fumes from a mower, and lately with traps. Very little success, and no hint of intimidation on the part of the moles.

Even beyond the confines of the garden, I've had problems with animals. I find it difficult to feel friendly toward beavers, which in New England are capable of riparian ruin greater than you would expect from their amiably lumpish buck-toothed appearance (ruin that the wildlife lobby in the UK now seems determined to inflict upon the British wilderness; reintroduction has already begun after centuries of beaverless peace and quiet). Trout fishing in bear country in the Rocky Mountains calls for armed defence – pepper spray and constantly singing or whistling is the order of the day. (So far the bears have kept their distance from me, I'm glad to say, and rattlesnakes likewise.)

Comparatively speaking, the beasts we contend with at home do not present quite the same mortal threat as bears and rattlesnakes, although to hear certain thoroughly beset gardeners complain you might think they did. In New England woodchucks caused a major amount of trouble, in spite of their peaceable nature. Woodchucks, for those unfamiliar with them, are stocky little beasts about the size of a large pan loaf. Also known as groundhogs, they will snack on the occasional worm or beetle but are basically herbivorous, which makes them a true garden menace. A stout chicken wire fence will keep them at bay, at least theoretically. That this is not infallible became clear to me one afternoon when I arrived to find a large woodchuck *inside* the fence, dining on French beans. I could not imagine how he got in there, given that the fence wire had a three-inch mesh and he was better than six inches wide. I found out. When he saw me, he promptly took a run at the fence, bounced off a couple of times, and then simply slithered through as if that three-inch mesh (or he) were made of rubber.

Then there are rabbits. I'm not sure where to begin with rabbits, except to say that for some reason, probably supernatural, I've never been much bothered by rabbits. In New England, rabbits were simply not a serious menace to anyone, possibly because most people let their dogs run around loose in our rural area. My fence kept them out of the vegetables in any case, even though I did not sink the bottom edge the requisite six inches into the ground. In Old England, the situation tends to be different – a friend in Essex tells me that he has had to give up gardening altogether because of a rabbit plague – but I remain unmolested. One fairly sound theory to explain my good fortune is the prevalence of foxes, all the more marked since the hunting ban came into force; apparently the anti-hunting crowd lacks the same sympathy for rabbits that it shows for foxes, which do seem to be multiplying. As for hares, there are some in the Welsh Marches, though not many – it's too wet – but I'm driven to conclude that hares do not pose a problem in our neighbourhood. Maybe they're unnerved by all the sheep.

I'm pleased to note that badgers and hedgehogs are also no bother to most of us, being too shy to harry the hostas or decimate the dicentra. Dairy farmers, convinced that badgers carry bovine tuberculosis, are less accommodating, and would prefer to see the entire species wiped out. I personally am far more pleased than chagrined to see a badger hirpling through the wood at dusk or to find a hedgehog curled in a spiky ball amid the nettles. Their diet of slugs and insects, if nothing else, should recommend them to every gardener.

On the other hand, there is nothing at all that can recommend a deer. To my despair, I know something about deer. Alford, where I used to live in the Berkshire Hills of Massachusetts, was simply full of deer. Per acre, it was reputed to have as many white-tail deer as any place in the United States. Seldom did a hunter venture into the Alford woods in deer season without coming back with his buck. And there were plenty of hunters, too, so many that they had to wear orange jackets to keep from shooting each other. But the number of deer never seemed to diminish. In winter you could be fairly certain to lose anything tall enough to stick up through the snow. (I still recall, with some pain, the destruction of a prized iberis border fronting a perennial bed.) And summer? Well, summer meant regular evasive measures like stringing creosote-soaked rope around that vegetable garden fence (it didn't work), and hoping that a greater human presence (including children running around outdoors) might discourage the worst ravages.

Still, of course, they came, sometimes at night, sometimes during the week when we were back in the city. You'd find their sign – little piles of dung, slots left by their hoofs in soft earth. I never built the recommended eight-foot fence – even deer don't deserve that kind of attention from me – settling instead for coexistence. They were pretty things, you could say that for them, certainly nicer to look at than woodchucks.

It's possible that I would have been more aggressive or experimental *vis a vis* deer back then if I'd known about a book that I came across just the other day. It's called, straightforwardly, *Gardens and Deer: A Guide to Damage Limitation.* Written by Charles Coles, a retired naval officer and wildlife expert who carried on his own war against deer in a garden on the edge of the New Forest, it summarises the results of a survey he conducted among some 300 British gardeners and offers practical advice. It would be nice to report that Coles found the magic bullet, as it were – he didn't – but he (and his correspondents) came up with some reasonably positive ideas apart from planting things that deer don't like to eat. (There do seem to be such things, although unanimity on what they are is rather lacking; Coles supplies a useful list of relatively deer-proof species ranging from primula to deutzia by way of daffodil, camellia, clematis, peony, alchemilla, mahonia, and – no surprise – holly. What's lacking, inevitably I suppose, are any authentically deer-proof vegetables.)

Deterrent ideas include bags of human hair, flashing lights, mothballs, rags dunked in creosote, dried blood, automatic security lights, and various sound generators. Dogs, sheep, cows and geese all made deer skittish, according to various of Coles's respondents – but not always. In fact, the real burden of *Gardens and Deer* seems to be that deer are unpredictable, and you just can't count on any dodge to work every time. Some work better than others, but it's impossible to tell which are which. The only surefire solution may be a rifle.

A recent story in *The New York Times* suggests that if deer really do keep increasing in Britain as they have been in the eastern United States, shooting indeed may be the only way out. In the densely-settled suburbs north of New York City, even conservation organizations like the Audubon Society have been calling for culls, pointing to extensive woodland areas where every sapling younger than 20 years has been browsed to the ground by deer. So far nothing like this has happened in my neighbourhood near Monmouth, but the other day I spotted a herd of delicately spotted fallow deer ambling through the apple orchard, so it may be only a matter of time. The distribution maps in *Gardens and Deer* (which, published a dozen years ago, is now a bit out of date) indicate that the five species of deer found in Britain (roe deer, fallow deer, muntjac, red deer and sika) were already depressingly widespread – and they didn't have many enemies.

It might be otherwise. A few days ago, in the middle of Washington, D. C., visitors to the National Zoo were startled to see a deer wander in from Rock Creek Park and jump the fence into the lions' enclosure. That was the end of the deer. Now if we were prepared to offer our marauding and all-too-fecund deer some real competition in the form natural antagonists such as lions, the problem might be solved. It's a long shot, I admit.

Why Every Man Needs a Tractor

I make no secret of my affection for machines. I'm not troubled in the least by the noise or the fumes, although to preserve my credentials in a society where such effluvia are frowned upon I sometimes claim to be concerned. I go along with the principle that a good machine ought not make a nuisance of itself. Most of mine don't.

So the big string trimmer, the hedge clippers, the mowers and the rototiller all have a useful happy existence at Towerhill Cottage. Even the leaf blower, whose utility has been rightly questioned (the wind does at least as good a job gathering leaves) gets a friendly glance of approbation from me now and then. In some not wholly reprehensible way, machines represent my kind of gardening.

There is one machine, however, which has proved to be rather more difficult to assimilate in my little gas-guzzling family.

A couple of years ago we were visiting a friend in Vermont when I first saw a compact tractor. It was a lovely thing, bright red, not too big, but substantial enough to do serious work. It had a front-end loader capable of lifting an amazing weight of stones or gravel or sand; in the rear there was a power take-off to which, my friend explained, you could attach a variety of auxiliary equipment from a plough to a brush cutter. The day we arrived he was just finishing up mowing a meadow. I watched him disconnect the mower and drive the tractor into its own little New England barn. My heart leaped with longing.

Back home, I thought about it. I didn't really *need* a tractor – who does? – but I couldn't get it out of my mind. It was partly the size of the thing, not exactly miniature but simply scaled down somehow, bigger and much more tractor-like than a ride-on mower, without being excessively agricultural. I could tell myself that it would be useful, which is more than could be said for antique cars, another category of machine that had charmed and tempted me (fortunately unsuccessfully) for years.

In retrospect, I suppose this would have been a good time to forget the whole cockamamie idea. For a while I did. But then one day, while looking for something else on the Internet, I came across an entire book entitled *Compact Tractor Buying Basics*, which you could download for a tenner or so. I read this hungrily, and the next thing I knew I was poring over tractor magazines and studying small ads listing machines for sale.

It wasn't clear sailing. I still had enough self-control to realize that I'd probably best stick to a used tractor, although I did go so far as to look at a new John Deere compact, and to an equally pristine Chinese model that a dealer in Herefordshire had mysteriously started to import. The John Deere was certainly beautiful, but cost about £14,000; the Siromer was splendidly painted bright red and cost considerably less, but even to my untutored eye it was clear that the engineering left a lot to be desired. Besides, I was beginning to learn something about tractors – and there was a depressingly large amount to learn.

When you are looking for something like a tractor, it's natural to go to the Internet and browse. The first thing I discovered was that next to video games and porn, just about nothing else is discussed in the cyberworld with such enthusiasm, assiduity and sheer loquaciousness as tractors. People (men) with tractors just love to talk about them. They love to tell you what their tractors can do and how much they cost, how to fix them and keep them running, where to get parts and accessories, which brands to buy and which to avoid. I found out why Western countries are flooded with scarcely used Japanese compact tractors (government tax policies there force rice farmers to buy new after only a year or two, resulting in a large number of otherwise unsaleable machines being shipped overseas). I also learned why these otherwise perfectly attractive 'grey market' tractors can be a problem to purchasers – in cases where manufacturers have set up their own sales operations in foreign countries, they don't relish the idea of being undercut by cheap imports carrying the same brand name. Apart from bringing lawsuits against the importers, they won't sell you parts and generally regard you with contempt if you need servicing. And then there was the galaxy of brand names to sort out, most of them Japanese or Chinese (Hinomoto, Komatsu, Shibaura, Kioti, Kubota, Siromer, Foton, Benye, Shire) and even an Indian (Mahindra) or two.

I ought to have been discouraged, but wasn't. On the outskirts of Bristol I located a muddy one-time farmyard converted into an outdoor tractor saleroom. It was lined with plausible machines, all clearly oriental (whatever safety stickers that weren't already worn off were in Japanese or Chinese). Dazed, I put down a deposit on a Kubota with a front-end loader. It really looked the part – four-wheel drive, orange paint job still bearing the traces of mud from a Shikoku paddy, a diesel engine that roared into life with very little prompting from the salesman. It could be delivered by the weekend. I went home to wait, wondering whether I had been a little precipitate.

As it turned out, I had been. On the night before it was to arrive, I found that a neighbour had an identical but even better Kubota to sell, not a 'grey market' import but the real thing, at a considerably lower price. Leaving the Bristol dealer annoyed (but partly mollified by the deposit, which he kept), I struck a deal with the neighbour, who agreed to drive it over as soon as he finished grading his new back garden. A couple of weeks later I had it parked under an apple tree in the orchard: a B1750 Kubota, 760 hours on the clock (you measure tractor usage in hours, not miles), 20 horsepower diesel engine, a roll-over bar, even lights and a horn.

So at last I had a tractor of my own. The only thing lacking was a good reason for having it.

My first venture was to the wood, to grub up a stump. This proved to be hopeless; the tyres (nearly smooth so-called 'turf' tyres meant for use on golf courses) spun in the mud, while the front-end loader refused to dig in. I had better luck spreading out a fresh load of gravel for the drive, but an attempt to move a pile of manure again came to nothing because of the slippery tyres. The obvious solution was a set of 'ag' (agricultural) tyres with bar lugs. Pricey, but necessary.

I bought them. Now, at least, I could get a grip, although one consequence was deep, permanent ruts wherever I cruised – through the orchard, across the meadow, into the wood. The cost was adding up, too. The battery died, requiring replacement, and I started to worry about leaving the tractor parked outdoors in the Welsh rain. What I needed was some sort of shed. I remembered my friend's barn in Vermont – wouldn't it be nice to have a small barn like that to keep the tractor in? Something simple and cheap.

This idea gave rise to a lot of sketching and cogitation and consultation with builders. We needed a potting shed; adding that onto the side of the little barn seemed logical at the time, although this meant raising the main roof high enough to create a second floor. And if there was going to be a second floor, then I really had to increase the dimensions of the building in order to get the proportions right. No point in being chintzy, as we say in Michigan.

The result, six months later, was big and beautiful. Very big. I'm still admiring it. The potting shed is elegant and the tractor is comfortably protected from the elements. The one drawback, probably predictable, is that the structure ended up costing roughly four times as much as the tractor had.

I'd like to be able to claim that I've discovered all sorts of exciting new uses for my little Kubota, apart from feeding it money. I did manage to move a couple of tons of building stone with reasonable efficiency, and lifted two or three large bags of sand out of the driveway where a builder had left them. An attempt to hook up a log splitter ended in failure when I learned that the extra hydraulics supplied for implements attached to the rear end lacked the necessary pressure, and in any case drove the splitter wedge in only one direction. The battery, short on charging, is generally dead. Nevertheless, once a year come August, when I jump-start the engine, borrow a big field mower, and get out there to chug around the meadow topping the thistles, there's a thrill that none of my other machines can quite match. I'm inclined to persist. I'm bound to find something else to do with it.

Time and the Garden

Clearing weeds from the flagstone terrace the other day, I noticed that the pergola seemed to be subsiding. The cross-beams, rather too heavily festooned with clematis montana, were no longer level, and the pillars, which I'd built out of four-by-four treated timber, were mysteriously shorter, as if some leviathan with a sledge had driven them deeper into the ground. This was disconcerting, to say the least. What I discovered was that the pillars had in fact started to sink, the cause being a combination of rot and simple gravity. When I put up the pergola about a dozen years ago, I had planted the pillars straight into the earth on the assumption that it was the best way to make the whole edifice stable. Stable it was, at least until recently, but I failed to take account of the fact that even the best-treated timber is mortal when soaked in rainwater (and snow) for a decade or so.

At the moment, I am still waiting for the pergola to give up the ghost and collapse. Its days are clearly numbered. The clematis will most likely deliver the quietus; you can discern a kind of savage exultation in the way it sends new tendrils racing across the now-delicate structure, as if sensing that victory is at hand. I'll be sorry to see the old thing go – it has been the scene of many happy summer lunches in the dappled shade beneath it – but it's probably time to think of replacing it with something more permanent.

It may be because I am myself gingerly approaching my ninth

decade on earth that I find myself pondering this matter of permanence and time and decay. I haven't begun to obsess about it, mind you, though that may come; so far my consideration is limited to the garden. It's engaging to think about such things during those spells of mental vacancy that accompany such activities as weeding the herbaceous border or mowing the orchard. Someone more disciplined than I am might actually work out a solid philosophical position explaining and justifying the function of time in the garden, which I don't want to do even if I could. I'm satisfied with a few observations.

When I was an editor I published some books on gardening. One was by a distinguished landscape designer, an American, who had the idea of choosing his one hundred favourite trees and shrubs, describing them and explaining how they could be best used in various garden situations, particularly in terms of design. Being at that time an extremely innocent and inexperienced gardener myself, I really had no business giving him editorial advice on a level more advanced than the correct use of gerunds, but I conceived that it was my duty to press him on bigger issues. So I tried to get him to say something about how we should also consider what was likely to happen to his designs as the plants grow and change over time. After all, if such planning aims at creating something to be distinctive and beautiful at a given moment, then you have to account for the fact that with living things there will be many moments, all different. The elements of your design will be in effect constantly in motion in relation to each another. A small shrub usually gets bigger, but not necessarily at the same speed as its neighbour.

I was sorry (but not awfully surprised) that my author didn't respond to my proposal. Maybe he didn't get the point, or regarded it as otiose. I suppose that an experienced horticulturalist knows instinctively how to contend with growth rates and making his scheme come together as it should, just as an experienced cook knows how to get the potatoes to the table at the same time as the chops. Like so much else it's something you learn, sooner or later, if you just stick with it long enough. But I still wish he had gone into the matter a bit. I continue to be mystified, especially when I try to understand practically anything about design.

Of course growth rates are only one aspect of time in a garden, and maybe not even the most important. There is also the antithetical and possibly perverse urge toward permanence.

When I first came to England, and we bought our ruinous cottage on the edge of Wales, I was moved (I almost said forced) to begin thinking in terms of stone. The house was stone, the barn I had built (to replace a collapsing corrugated iron shed) was cement block and stone, there were flagstones scattered around what was left of the garden. Tiny quarries punctuated the hillsides round about, and if you dug more that eighteen inches into the earth, you hit clay that was well on its way to being sandstone. So it was natural that our landscaping, such as it was, should make use of plenty of stone.

I built a long dry-stone retaining wall. I laid a terrace of flagstones, retrieving them from various collapsed sheds and buying others – one worn batch came from the old Monmouth police station and must has seen a lot of excitement over the course of a few centuries. I built raised beds and a platform where the pergola would be installed. I built a set of curving steps. And when I was done I had every reason to think that I had achieved something close to permanence. Not for me the wooden decking or the railroad ties; this stuff was made to *last*.

Looking back over the space of fifteen or twenty years, I can see that I was wrong. Not entirely wrong – the stones are still there – but time has done its work. The flagstone terrace, levelled on a bed of sand, now produces a sensational crop of weeds between the tilting flags; neither spraying nor assiduous scraping with a sort of flat metal hook keeps them down for more than a month or so. The wall is bulging suggestively in several places and the capstones are loose, undermined by ivy. The stones of the steps also persist in coming loose, probably because of frost and my ignorance of the principles of masonry. The base of the doomed pergola has become so uneven that you might think moles have invaded (and perhaps they have). Permanent it ain't.

On occasion I've been upset about this. I liked to think that what I've built ought to match the house (which has been braving the winds up the Bristol Channel for close on 200 years) in longevity, if not in beauty. But I'm gradually coming round to the conclusion that nothing in a garden is really permanent, or should be. Seriously hard landscaping constructed by professionals may have its place, but not around me. My wall may bulge, but it has the most beautiful lichens growing on it. The same goes for the uneven flagstones. And if it proves necessary to decapitate a gargantuan viburnum to keep it from doing violence to a meek but attractive hydrangea, well, that's life.

There are those – my wife is one of them – who quite happily keep updating the garden, making cuttings, adding new plants, getting rid of old exhausted specimens. Year by year, in the spirit of a creative gardener, she happily reduces overcrowding and fills the gaps wherever they occur with fresh species. Personally I find this approach difficult to follow, which I suppose defines me as conservative (or lazy). The border I originally planted fifteen years ago and tend to maintain still has most of the same plants (though they have moved around a bit, largely on their own). Some, like the globe thistles, got out of hand and had to be chopped mercilessly; others, like the monarda, have fought an increasingly unsuccessful battle against compost-borne weeds. The artichokes are beginning to look too big, as is a euonymus alatus that expands so handsomely and greenly in the spring that I can't bear to cut it back. In any case, I quite like the idea of no change.

But of course no change is really not an option. The world is full of lost gardens, every one of which descended into oblivion through its own irrepressible desire for change, its urge toward dissolution. A garden can no more defeat time than it can be truly natural, and the best the gardener can hope to do is manage the inevitable. I'm willing to go along with this – have I any choice? – but in the meantime, let's take it slow.

INDEX